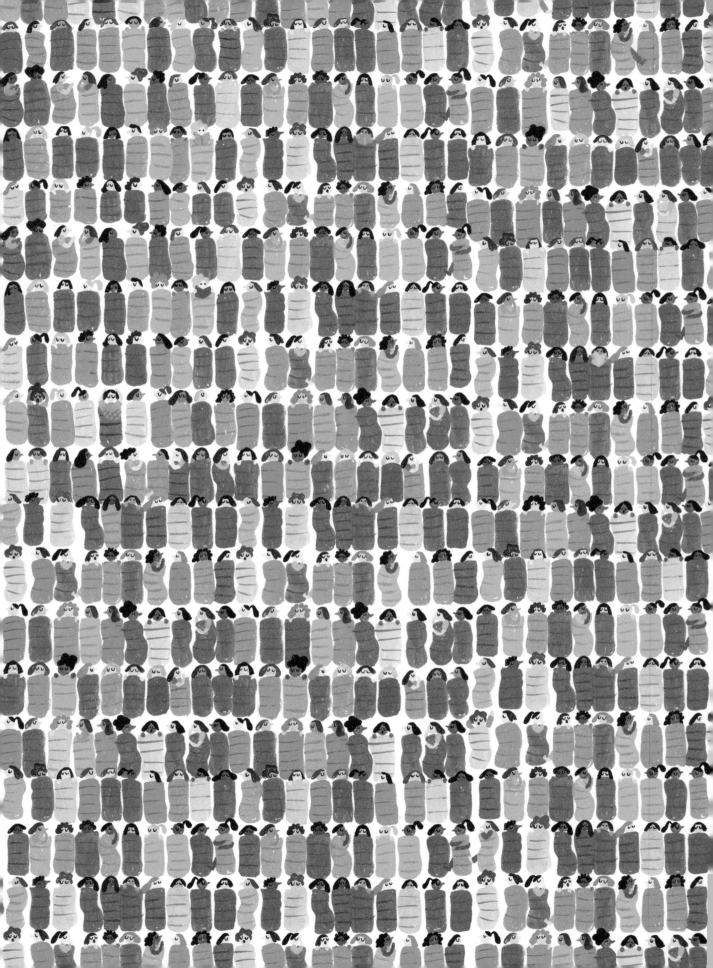

5
Minute
Really True
Stories for Bedtime

5 Minute
Really True
Stories for Bedtime

**BRITANNICA
BOOKS**

Contents

Why Do We Sleep? 6

What Are Dreams? 14

Heading to Bed 20

Sleeping Champions! 22

Record-breaking Beds 30

King Tut's Beds 38

Beds Around the World 46

Warm as Toast! 52

Asleep in Space 54

Rock-a-bye Sleeping 60

Sleeping on the Move 64

A Busy Night at the Hospital 70

Find it, Fix it! 76

The Rush to Market 80

Night Hunters 86

The Great Sleep Escape 94

Watery Beds 102

How Do They Sleep? 110

A Grizzly Bear's Winter 118

Remarkable Hibernators 126

Sunrise to Sunset 134

The Midnight Sun 140

The Northern Lights 146

A Trip to the Stars 150

Stargazing 156

Stories in the Stars 160

I See the Moon 166

Fly Me to the Moon 172

Moon Mysteries 178

Lullabies Around the World 182

Meet the Authors & Illustrators 186

Glossary 188

Sources 189

Index 190

Why Do We Sleep?

We all spend *a lot* of our time snoozing. In fact, children sleep for almost half of their lives. Why? It's because our bodies need it. Sleep is just as important as food and exercise.

Yawn!

When you're tired, your eyes feel heavy and you start to yawn.

Have you ever wondered why we sleep at nighttime instead of in the daytime? You can't see it, but your body has a clock that matches the Sun, and it can tell when it's night and when it's day. As night comes and it gets darker, your brain tells you it's time for sleep. But we're not all exactly the same when it comes to bedtime . . .

Larks wake early to sing their songs.

Chirp! Chirp!

Some of us like to go to sleep early and wake up early in the morning. These people are sometimes called larks because larks wake up and start singing by sunrise.

Others like to go to bed late and then sleep later in the morning. They are often called night owls because owls are nocturnal, meaning they are active at night.

Which one are you?

Hoot! Hoot!

Owls come out at night.

So, what exactly is sleep? It's a natural state of rest, where your awareness of what's happening around you gets turned right down. There are several different stages of sleep, which repeat through the night.

3
We dream during
Rapid Eye Movement (REM) sleep.

2
We relax further: our body temperature drops,
our breathing becomes regular, and we enter deep sleep.
This is when our body recovers from the day.

1
It takes around seven minutes for most of
us to go from wakefulness to light sleep.

Most people have a favorite sleeping position. Here are some of the most popular poses. How do you like to sleep? Do you stay in one spot or wriggle around into lots of different positions?

Soldier

Free-faller

Starfish

Fetus

Log

Yearner

Sleep affects every part of your body in the most incredible ways. Your brain even gets cleaned while you sleep! Here are some of the other things that a good night's sleep helps with.

Calms your emotions

Helps you remember new skills

Shapes the events of the day into memories

Fights infections

Keeps your heart healthy

Heals your skin

Helps your nails grow

Helps bones and muscles grow strong

11

Lots of other funny things can happen while you sleep . . .

Woah!

Snore!

Nearly all children snore some of the time, especially when they have a cold, and one in ten children snores every night. It happens when something blocks the air going to your throat. It might be your tongue or your airways, which relax as you sleep, that vibrate like a musical instrument.

Have you ever had a strange feeling that you're falling out of bed? This sometimes happens as you're falling asleep and jerk awake. It's called a hypnic jerk. Scientists think this happens because, as our muscles relax, our brain gets confused and thinks we're falling, so it tries to catch itself.

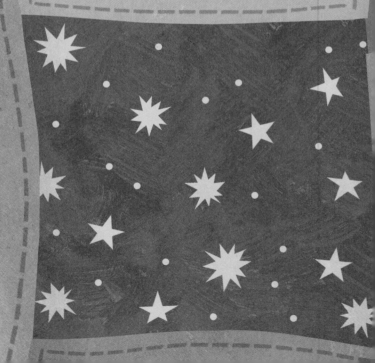

Chit- chat!

Children tend to talk in their sleep much more than adults do. Sometimes sleep talkers make perfect sense. You can even have a conversation with them! But if a sleep talker is in very deep sleep, they usually talk gibberish.

About 15 percent of children sleepwalk, and it happens more if you're not getting enough sleep. Sometimes children just sit up in bed. Sometimes they walk all around the house.

What Are Dreams?

Dreams are mysterious things. They are pictures and stories created by our minds while we're sleeping. Sometimes they're fascinating, sometimes scary, and sometimes just plain weird!

You have as many as seven dreams each night. Scientists think that even babies growing in their mothers' wombs might dream. We forget nearly all of our dreams. The funny thing is, we are most likely to remember one if we wake up in the middle of it.

It's difficult to study dreams, so there's still a lot we don't understand. Scientists are trying to figure out exactly what dreams are for.

We dream during a type of sleep called REM, or Rapid Eye Movement sleep. This is what happens:

Your eyes move quickly under your closed eyelids.

Your legs and arms can't move, and it's a good thing they can't. You wouldn't want to act out your dreams!

Your breathing becomes faster.

Your heart beats faster.

When you first go to bed your dreams might last just a few minutes, but towards the end of the night you can dream for up to half an hour. The place where the most fascinating stuff happens, however, is in your brain.

It might look like a bunch of pink sausages, but this is your brain! All parts of your brain are active while you dream, but one area is especially busy. It's called the limbic system, and it controls your emotions, such as anger, sadness, and happiness. This might be why we often dream about times when we've had strong feelings.

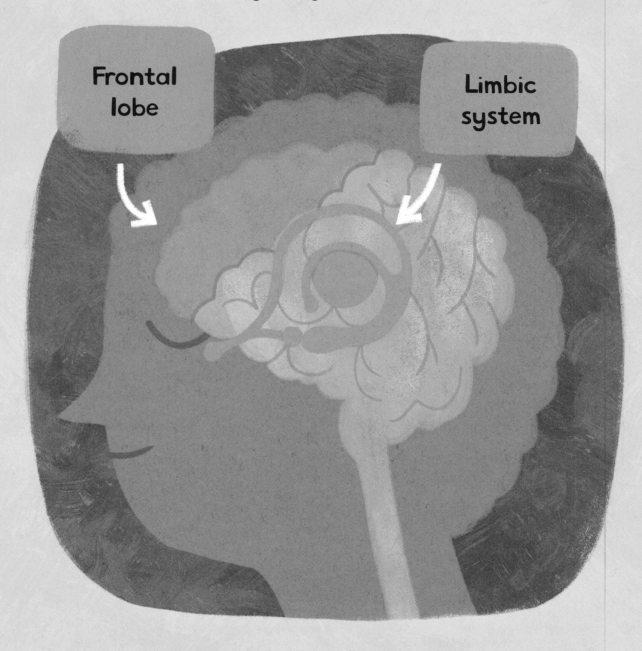

The frontal lobe is the "sensible" part of the brain. This area is quieter while we dream, which could explain why our dreams can be weird.

So the brain is very busy when we dream—but it's busy in a different way from when we're awake. Scientists think that during sleep, the brain is connecting the things we've learned that day with everything else we've ever known. This could be why we can suddenly solve a difficult problem when we wake up!

"Yesterday" by the Beatles is one of the most successful songs ever written. And it started as a dream! Paul McCartney dreamt the melody, woke up, and rushed to his piano before he forgot it. Think what you might do with inspiration from your dreams.

This page, from an Egyptian dream book, can be found in the British Museum in London, U.K. It's a bit ragged, but then it is 3,200 years old!

People have always been fascinated by dreams and their meanings. The ancient Egyptians believed that dreams were sent by the gods. They went to dream temples to ask for dreams that would help them solve their problems. But dream messages weren't easy to understand. Some people even kept books of their dreams to figure out what they meant.

The Bible has many examples of dreams telling people about the future. One famous story is about Joseph, who wore a colorful coat and could interpret dreams.

In ancient China, people used a book called *Duke of Zhou Interprets Dreams* to see what their dreams meant. If someone dreamt of a tiger or a snake, it was considered lucky.

Dreamcatchers are thought to originally have been made by the Ojibwa people of Canada and the United States. They hang dreamcatchers above their beds and believe that dreams will get caught in the web. Dreamcatchers let good dreams slide down to the person sleeping below and trap bad dreams, which get destroyed in the morning by sunlight.

Electrodes

EEG display

Scientists try to better understand dreams by using a machine called an EEG. It can measure what happens in the dreaming brain. Maybe one day someone will invent a dream-reading machine.

Heading to Bed

Children need much more sleep than grown-ups do. That's because children are growing and their brains are developing all the time. Are you going to bed at the right time to get enough sleep? Check out how long scientists recommend you spend in the land of nod . . .

0–12 months: up to 17 hours

1–2 years: 11–14 hours

3–5 years: 10–13 hours

14–17 years: 8–10 hours

6–13 years: 9–11 hours

Grown-ups: 7–9 hours

We can do lots of things to get a better night's sleep. Exercising during the day is helpful. It's best not to eat chocolate close to bedtime because it has caffeine in it, which can keep you awake. It's also a very good idea to take time to relax before bed.

Put electronics away before bedtime. Their blue light can trick your brain into thinking it's daytime, which stops you from sleeping well.

A hot bath helps because it cools you down. How strange! Hot water makes blood rush to your skin. This cools your body, helping you to sleep better.

Reading a book is an excellent way to relax, especially reading this one!

Puzzles are good for calming your mind.

Try to go to bed around the same time every night.

Listening to a lullaby can help you calm down and drift off to sleep.

Can you think of other things that help you relax? How about counting sheep? We used to think this would help us sleep, but scientists discovered that it doesn't! They found it's better to imagine going on a nice walk, maybe along a beach or through the woods. Where would you go on your imaginary walk?

Sleeping Champions!

Are you the fastest runner in your school? Or maybe you're the loudest, the strongest, or have the longest hair. That's amazing! But what if you were the best in your country, or even better, in the whole world?

Then you might find your name in the *Guinness World Records*. It's full of people and things that hold the record for being the best ever at something. Most records take people a lot of time, practice, and energy to achieve. For others, well, it's just something they do in their sleep.

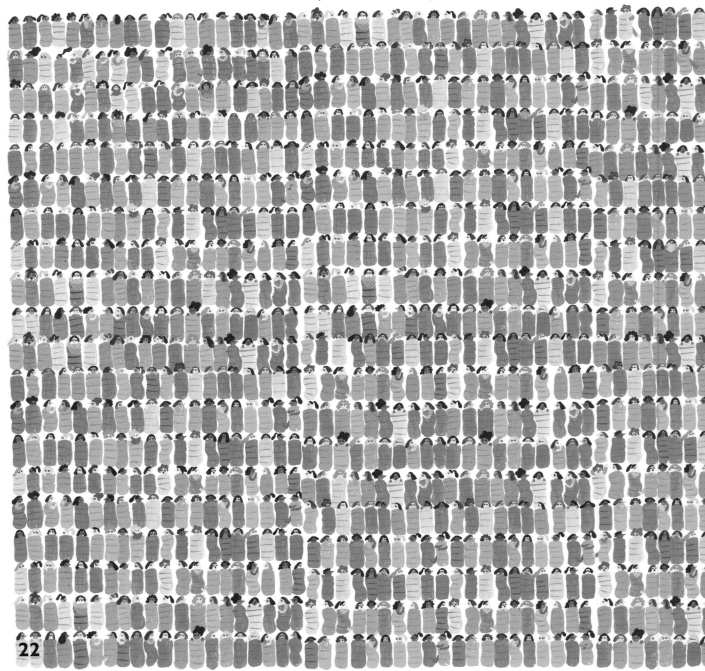

On September 27, 2014, in Cheshire, U.K., 2,004 Girl Scouts gathered in a giggling girl-gaggle to hold the largest ever sleepover. And what better place to do it than in a huge tent at the zoo? The deal was that the girls had to sleep for at least five hours if they were to snatch the existing world record from 1,626 Girl Scouts in Kent, also in the U.K. The pressure was on! Officials from Guinness World Records made sure that the girls followed the rules and the next morning declared the seven- to ten-year-olds world record holders!

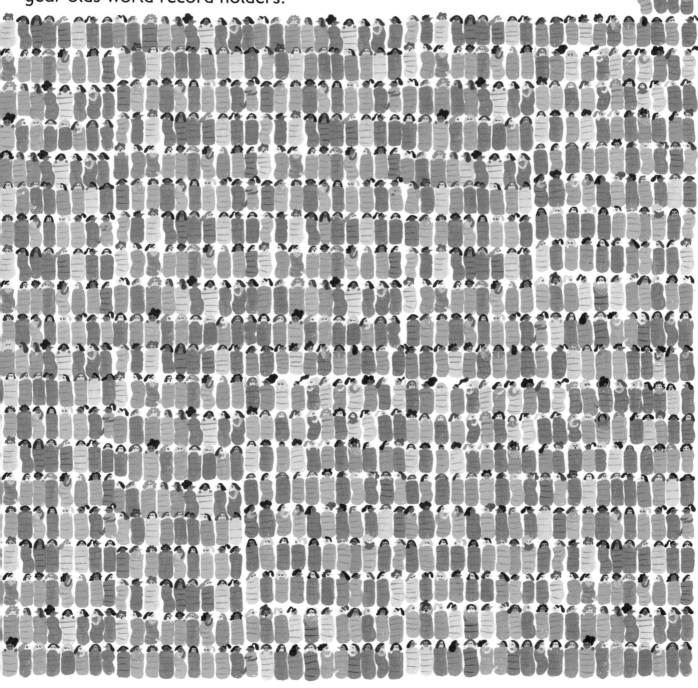

Have you ever taken a catnap? You probably have—a catnap is when you have a little doze during the day, just like a cat. Cats sleep for about 15 hours a day. How lazy is that? But it doesn't even begin to compare with the sleepiest world record holder of all time—the little brown bat. Shhh, don't wake it up!

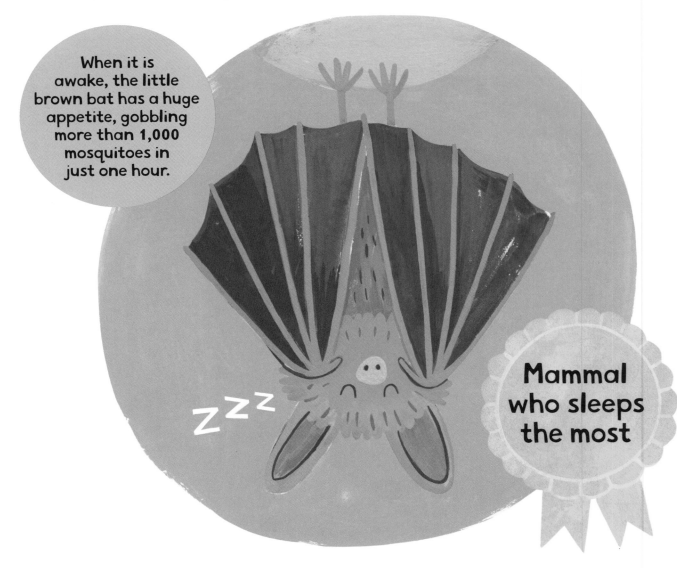

When it is awake, the little brown bat has a huge appetite, gobbling more than 1,000 mosquitoes in just one hour.

Mammal who sleeps the most

This tiny mammal hangs out in caves and forests in North America. And it's not called the *little* brown bat for nothing. It is only about 3.5 inches (9cm) long—that's about the same length as a crayon. It doesn't weigh much more than a crayon either. However, for such a small creature, it certainly takes the biggest snooze. This bat spends almost 20 hours a day in the land of nod.

The mammal who gets the least shut-eye of all is . . . trumpet fanfare, please . . . the African elephant!

In 2016, scientists studied two wild elephants in southern Africa to find out more about how these huge creatures sleep. By placing special trackers under the skin of their trunks, scientists discovered that the elephants slept for only two hours a day. Sometimes they didn't sleep at all! How the elephants stay healthy with so little sleep is still a mystery.

Mammal
who sleeps
the least

On August 6, 1961, Gherman Titov from Russia was having a hard time falling asleep. Why? He was suffering from motion sickness—which was not surprising. At the time, he was looping Earth on his Soviet spacecraft, Vostok 2!

First person to sleep in space

As he tried to sleep, the queasy cosmonaut—that's the Russian version of an astronaut—was disturbed by his hands floating above his body in the weightless environment. After tucking his loose limbs under his belt, Titov finally fell asleep.

By the end of his mission, he had managed to orbit Earth a total of 18 times and to break an extra-gross world record at the same time. In addition to being the first person to sleep in space, Titov was also the first to vomit there. Yuck!

The official world record for the loudest snore is held by Kåre Walkert, who grunted and snored his way into the *Guinness World Records* in Sweden in 1993. His snore was recorded as 93 decibels, which is as loud as a lawn mower!

But a woman in the U.K. has beaten that record. She was recorded snoring at a whopping 111.6 decibels—that's noisier than a low-flying jet! The snore came from the mouth of Jenny Chapman, a grandmother who admits she's been a champion snorer for as long as she can remember.

A decibel is the way we measure noise. The lower the decibel number, the quieter the noise. So 10 decibels is as quiet as a rustling leaf, and 110 decibels is as loud as an ear-splitting chainsaw.

U.K.'s loudest snorer

Her husband says that sleeping in the same room with Jenny is like sleeping in a zoo. This is how he describes her different snores: "There's one that's like the roar of a lion, one that's like the trumpet of an elephant, and sometimes she does that thing that orangutans do." Maybe it's time someone invented the world's most powerful earplugs?

Record-breaking Beds

Would you like to sleep in the world's biggest bed? Maybe you'd prefer to snuggle under the largest patchwork quilt? From a sparkling bed covered in jewels to a grassy mattress in a cave, all of the beds in this amazing collection hold world records.

How comfortable is your bed? Chances are, you have a pretty good mattress to lie on in a warm, dry home. But imagine living in a dark, damp cave thousands of years ago before beds were invented. What would you have slept on?

The answer can be found at a cave site in KwaZulu-Natal, South Africa, where scientists have discovered the world's oldest bed. Well, it's more like a mattress made from grasses and leafy plants, squashed down to create a very comfy, springy surface. And the clever, bed-making humans from long ago topped it off with leaves from a tree that repels insects, probably to stop lice and mosquitoes from biting them while they slept.

After digging into the 77,000-year-old mattress, the scientists were surprised to find that it was made up of layer upon layer of bedding. This meant that the humans regularly added new leaves and grasses to keep the bed fresh and bouncy.

World's oldest mattress

The scientists also discovered that when things got too dirty, the humans set fire to the bed to get rid of all the gross stuff before making it all over again.

The ancient, grassy mattress was big enough for a whole family to sleep on. And not only sleep—after finding stone tools and tiny pieces of bone, scientists think the cave family also ate their breakfast in bed!

Four-poster beds aren't beds with four posters pinned to them. They are beds that have posts on each of their four corners. These tall posts support a roof that has curtains hanging from it, and the curtains can be closed at night to create a cozy little room. Not many people have four-poster beds any more, and only very rich people had them in the past. If you were a rich person from the past, the curtained bed would have come in handy. Not only did it give you some privacy, but it also kept cold air out. How snuggly!

World's biggest four-poster bed

One story about the Great Bed says that 12 butchers and their wives slept in it.

The biggest and possibly the oldest four-poster bed is on display in the Victoria and Albert Museum in London, U.K. It is called the Great Bed of Ware and is big enough for eight grown-ups. Why would anyone build a bed so big? Well, in the 1590s, innkeepers in the town of Ware in Hertfordshire, U.K., wanted to attract travelers from London to come and stay. They asked a local carpenter to build the huge tourist attraction, and the inns took turns using it.

The bed became very famous and is mentioned in Shakespeare's play *Twelfth Night.*

Do you need a good, loooooong sleep? Then try sleeping in the biggest bed in the world! Made for the summer festival of St. Gregorius in Hertme in the Netherlands, it was about the same size as a basketball court!

World's biggest bed

And what could be more fitting for the biggest bed in the world than the world's biggest patchwork quilt? Made in Portugal in the year 2000, this quilt is called *Manta da Cultura*, which means "Patchwork for Culture." It takes up the same amount of space as three soccer fields!

Two dogs in Gloucestershire, U.K., have an extremely extravagant "woof" over their heads. In 2008, the owner of the Great Danes paid a whopping $498,000 for a luxury dog house, which has two bedrooms with temperature-controlled beds lined with snuggly covers. It also has a living room with a huge plasma television, an adventure play area, and a spa bath for pooch pampering.

Most expensive dog house

The most valuable, and possibly the most glitzy, bed in the world is covered with 802,903 Swarovski crystals. Unveiled in China in 2009, it is called the K.mooi Crystal Noir Limited Edition. If you would like to sleep on this sparkly dream bed, then dream on. It would cost $440,000, which is enough money to buy a house!

World's most valuable bed

So there you have it. A fine collection of world-record-breaking beds! Which one would you choose to snooze in? Sweet dreams wherever you decide to snuggle down. Maybe you'll break the record for the world's longest sleep!

King Tut's Beds

In ancient Egypt, kings were called pharaohs. It was believed that pharaohs were gods who lived on Earth. One of these god-kings was Tutankhamun (King Tut). He took the throne about 3,300 years ago at only nine years old and died about ten years later.

Ancient Egyptians believed that after anyone died, they went to another place and lived an afterlife. They also thought you could take things with you on the journey.

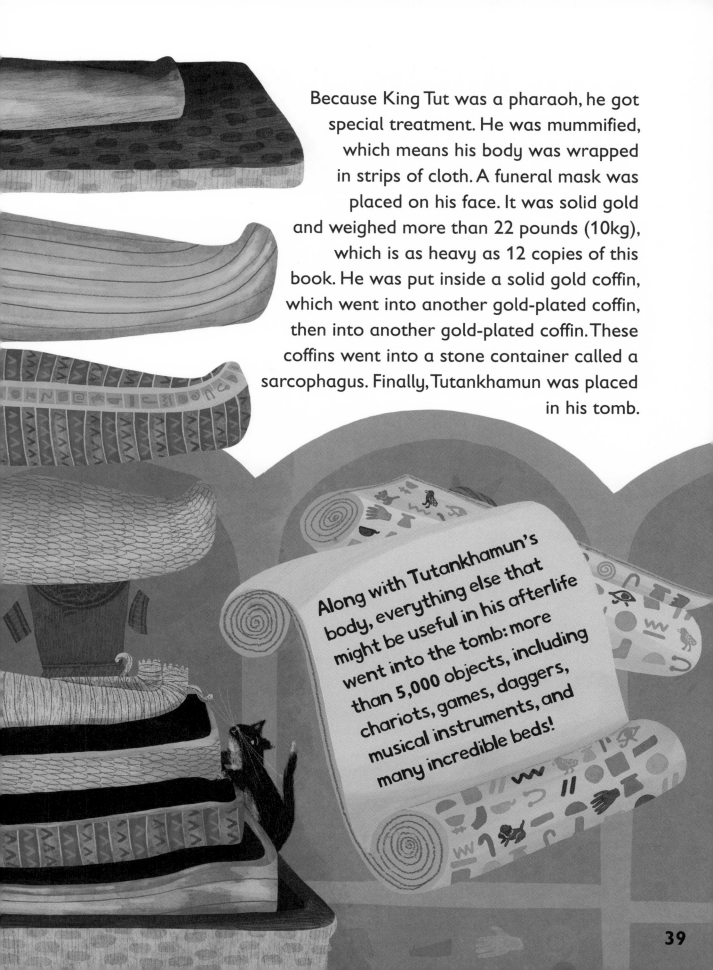

Because King Tut was a pharaoh, he got special treatment. He was mummified, which means his body was wrapped in strips of cloth. A funeral mask was placed on his face. It was solid gold and weighed more than 22 pounds (10kg), which is as heavy as 12 copies of this book. He was put inside a solid gold coffin, which went into another gold-plated coffin, then into another gold-plated coffin. These coffins went into a stone container called a sarcophagus. Finally, Tutankhamun was placed in his tomb.

Along with Tutankhamun's body, everything else that might be useful in his afterlife went into the tomb: more than 5,000 objects, including chariots, games, daggers, musical instruments, and many incredible beds!

The beds found in Tutankhamun's tomb were all different, and they were beautifully carved and decorated.

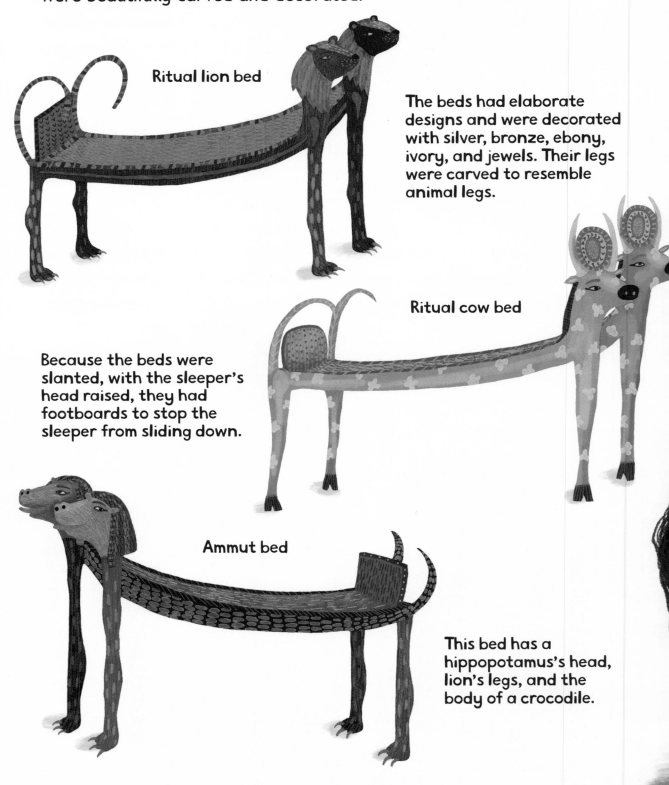

Ritual lion bed

The beds had elaborate designs and were decorated with silver, bronze, ebony, ivory, and jewels. Their legs were carved to resemble animal legs.

Ritual cow bed

Because the beds were slanted, with the sleeper's head raised, they had footboards to stop the sleeper from sliding down.

Ammut bed

This bed has a hippopotamus's head, lion's legs, and the body of a crocodile.

This ivory headrest shows the Egyptian god Shu with two sleepy lions sitting next to him.

Four special headrests were also found in Tutankhamun's tomb. They were made of ivory, gold, and glass.

Ancient Egyptians used headrests instead of pillows. They placed linen cushions on top to make them more cozy. The headrests allowed air to move around the sleeping person's neck and head, keeping them cool. They also protected the sleeper's fancy hairstyle and stopped creepy-crawlies from climbing onto their face.

One of the beds found in Tutankhamun's tomb is what is thought to be the very first Z-shaped cot. This means it folds up to look a bit like the letter Z. It was made especially for King Tut and is the only one to have been found in a tomb.

Despite being a cot, it was elegant, comfortable, and steady. Its legs were shaped into lion legs with paws. Ancient Egyptians liked the idea of powerful lions lifting them up as they sat or slept, so they often used lion legs for their furniture.

Tutankhamun might have taken this cot with him when he went hunting and camping. Earlier cots folded in half, but this one folded in thirds, making it smaller and easier for his servants to carry. (But it still looks pretty heavy.)

Tutankhamun might have had a cot for another reason, too. If he went on a tour of his land, he would have wanted a grand bed to sleep in. But not many people owned beds in ancient Egypt. They either had a mattress made of straw or they slept on a bed of palm leaves. And perhaps a pharaoh wouldn't have been very impressed by either of those choices!

Beds Around the World

Futon

A futon is a traditional Japanese bed. The word futon describes two parts: the thin *shikibuton*, which is the bottom mattress, and the *kakebuton*, which is a thick bedcover. You can fold up both parts in the morning and put them away in a closet. That's really handy if you don't have much space. Futons are often placed on a *tatami* mat. The mat is made of grass and rice straw, which adds a bit more comfy padding.

Charpoy

Charpoy means "four feet," which is exactly what this traditional bed from India has. The bed is often made from the wood of mango trees. The sleeping area is handwoven, and it's made of cotton, coconut fiber, or dried leaves. The loose weave allows air to flow up from below, keeping the bed nice and cool, which is perfect in a hot country like India.

Net bed

In parts of Africa, Asia, and Central and South America, people use mosquito nets to keep the pesky bugs away. Mosquitoes can spread diseases when they bite. What better way to keep them from nibbling you than to hang a net over your bed? It looks lovely, too.

Waterbed

A Scottish doctor first invented waterbeds for his patients in 1833. These waterbeds were like giant plastic cushions filled with warm water. And they were very wobbly: if you moved you'd make a wave inside the mattress! Some later versions have little pockets of water and air, which makes the beds much less wobbly.

Imagine sleeping high up in the air! The Korowai people, from a province called Papua in Indonesia, live in tree houses, high above mosquitoes that swarm near the damp ground. The tree houses have several rooms, with the men sleeping in one and the women in another. Each room has a fire for everyone to sleep around. This sounds a little dangerous in a wooden tree house, but the fire hangs above a hole, so if it gets out of control, it can quickly be dropped to the forest floor below. The Korowai beds are a thin slice of tree bark placed on wooden floorboards.

How about this for a bed? It's a Chinese wedding bed, which would be given as a gift when a couple was getting married. The beds were ornately carved with symbols to wish the happy couple many children and good luck. Several of these old beds still exist today, although the modern wedding beds are much simpler.

Chinese wedding bed

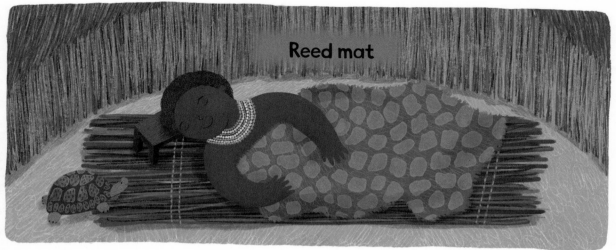

Reed mat

In South Africa, some Zulu people sleep in beehive-shaped huts called indlu. Traditionally they sleep on thin mats made of reeds on the floor of their huts, with animal skins to cover them. They use a small wooden bench as a headrest.

Igloo bed

You'd think it might be pretty chilly sleeping in an igloo, but they're surprisingly warm. Igloos are where the Inuit peoples of the far north stay when they go on hunting trips. They are built from bricks of snow and have several levels, with a fire on the middle one. The top level is the warmest, so that is where the Inuit sleep. They snooze on a mat of twigs and use thick animal furs as bedding.

What an amazing variety of beds there are! Where in the world would you like to sleep?

Warm as Toast!

Northern China has very long, freezing winters. Luckily, about 2,500 years ago a brilliant person came up with the idea of the Kang Bed-Stove, an ingenious invention that roasts your dinner as it toasts your toes. And it works so well that it's still being made and used today.

The word Kang means "dry," and the Kang Bed-Stove certainly helps keep moisture away. It heats up your whole house, you can cook on part of it, use it as a table or chair, and best of all, it's wonderfully warm to sleep on! The Kang Bed-Stove is a great place for families to come together during the day. They gather to talk, tell stories, sing, play games, and even get married. So how does the Kang Bed-Stove work?

This area closest to the stove is the warmest spot, so the eldest members of the family get to sleep here.

You light a fire in the stove. Wood, grass, coal, straw, and corn cobs are used to make the fire.

Cooking time! The stove cooks food and heats water for tea.

The heat from the stove goes through pipes under the bed.

The pipes look like a maze, which helps more heat to get close to the surface of the bed and warm it up!

The smoke from the fire is released outside through a chimney.

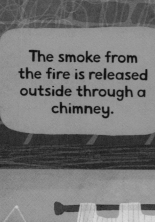

There's room for the whole family on the platform. Let's hope no one snores!

There is a layer of clay on top of the bricks. This is covered by straw matting, otherwise it would be too hot to sleep on. On top is a cotton-padded blanket and finally, a bed sheet.

A Kang table is sometimes put on the bed. It's useful for cups or food.

Traditional bedding similar to Japanese futons is rolled out at night and put away in the day, so family activities can take place.

There are sometimes drawers underneath, to dry out wet boots.

This platform is made from bricks. Bricks take a long time to heat up, but also a long time to cool down, so the bricks stay hot all night long, even if the fire goes out.

Asleep in Space

Imagine how it must feel to sleep in space. Probably very strange—you'd be far from home, spinning around Earth in a spacecraft, without normal gravity holding you down.

This is what it's like in the International Space Station (ISS), which is a huge spacecraft that orbits Earth once every 90 minutes. It's way up high—250 miles (400km) away—and it flies at about 17,500 miles (28,000km) an hour. Now that's fast!

European science lab behind the spacecraft

This spacecraft takes astronauts to and from Earth. Earth to **ISS** takes about six hours, but **ISS** to Earth only takes about three!

The astronauts' dining room

Sleeping cabins for four astronauts

U.S. science lab

This cupola has seven windows that the astronauts can look out of to see Earth.

The International Space Station was built by people from 15 different countries, for astronauts to work, live, and sleep in. You can sometimes see it from Earth without even using a telescope. It looks like a big white dot moving quickly across the night sky.

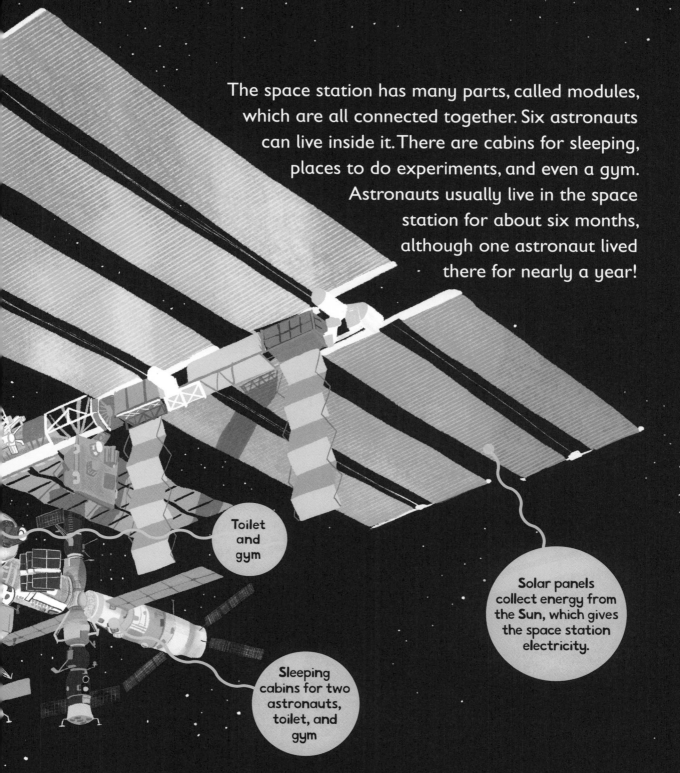

The space station has many parts, called modules, which are all connected together. Six astronauts can live inside it. There are cabins for sleeping, places to do experiments, and even a gym. Astronauts usually live in the space station for about six months, although one astronaut lived there for nearly a year!

Toilet and gym

Solar panels collect energy from the Sun, which gives the space station electricity.

Sleeping cabins for two astronauts, toilet, and gym

Astronauts are always busy. They make sure the space station is clean and working well. They sometimes go on spacewalks outside the station in their spacesuits. They also conduct many science experiments. This space research is used all the time in our everyday lives. So after all that hard work, the astronauts need a good night's sleep ...

But sleeping in a space station isn't as easy as sleeping on Earth. The space station travels so fast around our planet that it sees 16 sunrises and sunsets every day. This makes it hard for the astronauts' brains to know when it's time to go to bed. Plus, there is very little gravity in the space station, which means that everything, including the astronauts, floats. And because there is no "up" or "down," astronauts don't ever lie down to sleep. So they need to *train* their brains and bodies to sleep and wake up at the same time every day, with a strict routine.

First, exercise! It might be fun to float around all the time, but it's not good for the astronauts' muscles and bones, so it's very important that they exercise for two hours every day. Exercising during the day helps them sleep better. They can use a treadmill or a static bike, which they strap themselves to. They also have a weight machine to strengthen their muscles.

Astronauts have to eat well, too, and at regular times. Some of their food is dehydrated, or dried out. The astronauts add hot water to it before they eat.

How do astronauts stop their food from floating away? They keep it in containers, which are stuck to trays with Velcro—that's a fabric that is sometimes used to fasten shoes. The trays are also attached to a table with Velcro.

And just like us, astronauts need time to relax before bed. They can chat with family and friends using email or the telephone. They can read, listen to music, and play games—or just gaze at the incredible view.

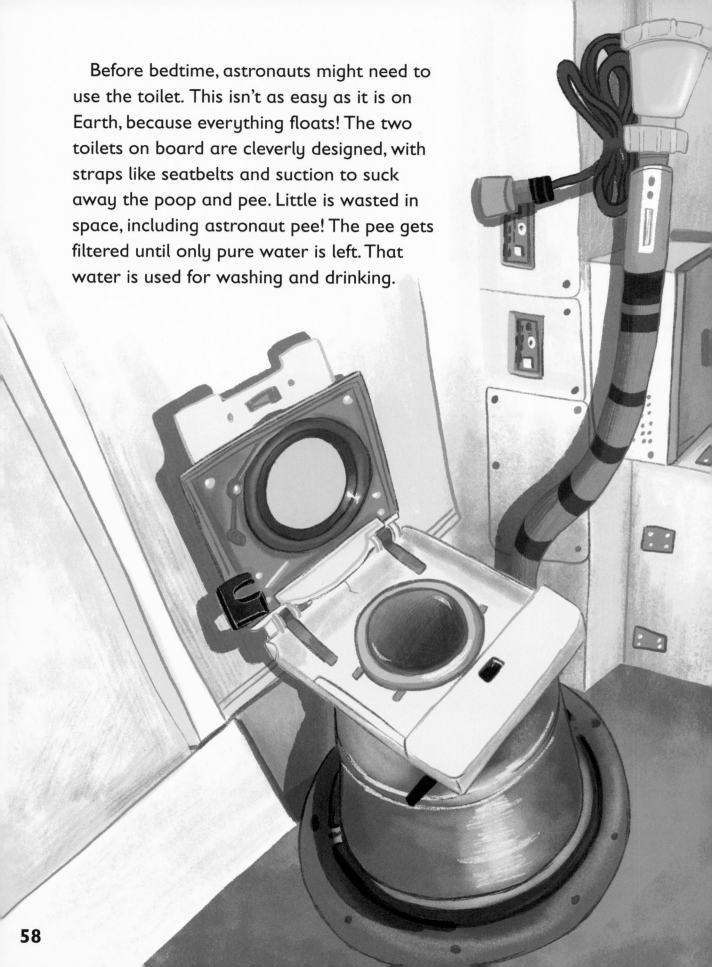

Before bedtime, astronauts might need to use the toilet. This isn't as easy as it is on Earth, because everything floats! The two toilets on board are cleverly designed, with straps like seatbelts and suction to suck away the poop and pee. Little is wasted in space, including astronaut pee! The pee gets filtered until only pure water is left. That water is used for washing and drinking.

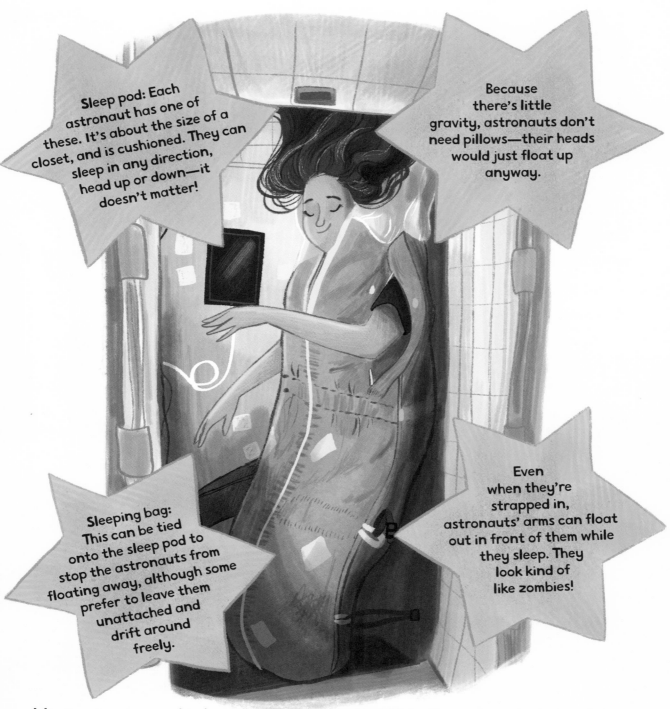

Sleep pod: Each astronaut has one of these. It's about the size of a closet, and is cushioned. They can sleep in any direction, head up or down—it doesn't matter!

Because there's little gravity, astronauts don't need pillows—their heads would just float up anyway.

Sleeping bag: This can be tied onto the sleep pod to stop the astronauts from floating away, although some prefer to leave them unattached and drift around freely.

Even when they're strapped in, astronauts' arms can float out in front of them while they sleep. They look kind of like zombies!

Most astronauts don't put on pajamas. Instead, they wear their work clothes at night and only change their underwear every other day. Their work shirts and shorts are changed every ten days. This is because they don't have much space for clothes, and with no washing machine on board, they have to make their clothes last a long time.

Sleeping in space isn't as straightforward as sleeping on Earth, but it sure looks like a whole lot of fun!

Rock-a-bye Sleeping

Is there anything more relaxing than drifting off to sleep in a hammock? Probably not! In fact, scientists have shown that lying in a swinging hammock affects our brains in a good way, helping us to fall asleep more quickly and sleep more deeply.

But hammocks aren't a new idea. Historians think they were first created more than a thousand years ago by people called the Maya, who live in Central America. The Maya still make hammocks today. To do this they use a loom made from tree branches, which looks like the one here.

Hammocks were a wonderful invention: comfortable, easy to hang, and they protected the Maya from snakes and biting ants on the ground.

Around 1590, sailors started using hammocks on ships. It was an excellent way to fit a lot of sailors into a small space. And the sailors must have been pleased. It's much better to be rocked above the waves than to sleep on a wet, hard ship deck.

Hammocks have always been handy for people traveling through jungles and forests. When it's time for bed, they string their hammocks in between trees, pop their rain cover over the top, and drift off to sleep!

At the International Highline Meeting Festival, held in Italy in September 2014, hundreds of people slept in hammocks attached to ropes which stretched across the Italian Alps, often 300 feet (90m) in the air. Don't worry, they wore harnesses in case they rolled over in bed!

Have you ever tried to get into a hammock and ended up on the floor? Embarrassing, isn't it? To keep your pride from being hurt (as well as your bottom), follow this very easy guide:

1. Stand halfway along one edge of the hammock, facing away from it.
2. Place your hands on the edge of the hammock, then sit down.
3. Make sure your bottom is in the center of the hammock.
4. Quickly swing your legs over the side and up into the hammock.
5. Shift yourself around, so you're lying diagonally across the hammock. Most people find this the most comfortable position.

Finally . . . never hang your hammock too tightly. It needs a good sag, like a happy, smiley face, to make it really comfy.

Sleeping on the Move

Have you ever slept in a bed on a train? You dash across the countryside and whizz through towns. Then, as the stars come out, you huddle down in your cozy bed and drift off to sleep to the clickety-clack of wheels on rails.

Sleeping on trains became very glamorous with the opening of the famous Orient Express line in 1883, which ran from Paris to Constantinople (now Istanbul, Turkey).

While you ate your dinner in the dining car, the attendant would flip your sofa into a fully made bed. The Orient Express line still runs today.

Overnight trains are becoming more and more popular. Not only are they better for our planet than airplanes, but there are some seriously cool trains all over the world. You can travel across Japan on the Shiki-shima, around Russia on the Golden Eagle, or through the Scottish highlands on the Royal Scotsman.

Trains are not the only way to snooze on the move. You can be rocked to sleep on the water, too. Narrowboats were working boats, first used more than 300 years ago in the U.K. They were pulled by horses and designed to travel along specially built waterways called canals. They transported lots of things, such as cement, or cheese, or sand, or sugar.

Working narrowboats used to be pulled by horses along a towpath, but now they have motors to power them.

These days there are still some working narrowboats, but mostly they are used for fun. By day, you sail along the water and, by night, you tie up your boat at the side of the canal. Then you snuggle down to sleep, maybe waking to a flock of ducks floating past your window!

How about sleeping under the sea? Life on a submarine is exciting, but there isn't much space. Sometimes there are more than 100 people squished together for 60 to 80 days at a time. It's hard to know when it's night and when it's day when you're deep underwater.

The submarine crew take turns working and sleeping. When one person wakes up, another person will go to sleep in the same bunk bed, drifting off to the humming of the submarine.

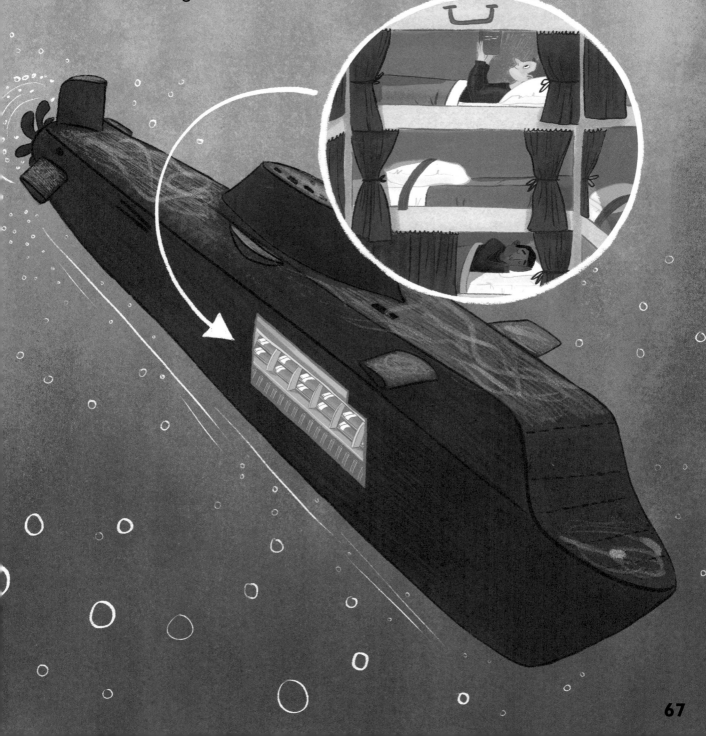

Musicians will sometimes snooze in a tour bus. They have a driver to take them from city to city, so that they can appear in performances all over the country. They might go to sleep in Maryland and wake up in Wisconsin, ready for their next concert.

Some tour buses have sides that slide outwards when parked, allowing more space for seating inside. Tour buses usually have curtained-off bunk beds—or private bedrooms and bathrooms if you're a really big star. They often have televisions, game consoles, and even a recording studio or a dance floor!

Most of us go to sleep and wake up in the same place, but what fun it would be to travel as you slumber. Boat, train, submarine, or super-bus . . . where in your wildest dreams would you like to snooze on the move?

A Busy Night at the Hospital

When you put on your pajamas, brush your teeth, and climb into bed, you may think that everyone else is going to bed, too. But as night falls, some people are getting ready for work. The world doesn't stop to rest, even at night! Fires start, babies are born, people want to eat, and they still need buses and taxis to get to where they need to go. And sometimes—accidents happen.

Then, it's time to go to the hospital, which is open all day and all night. Ambulance drivers pull up outside the Emergency Room, unlock the back doors, and paramedics jump out.

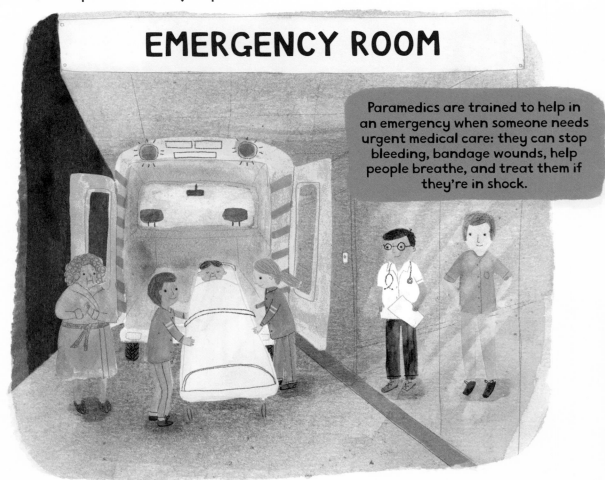

EMERGENCY ROOM

Paramedics are trained to help in an emergency when someone needs urgent medical care: they can stop bleeding, bandage wounds, help people breathe, and treat them if they're in shock.

The paramedics will gently lift a patient onto an ambulance stretcher and wheel them towards the hospital, where nurses and doctors working the night shift are waiting.

Inside the hospital, doctors and nurses decide on the best treatment for their patients. If a patient has a broken bone, they may need an X-ray. An X-ray is an image of the inside of your body. Hard bones show up white and soft parts show up dark gray.

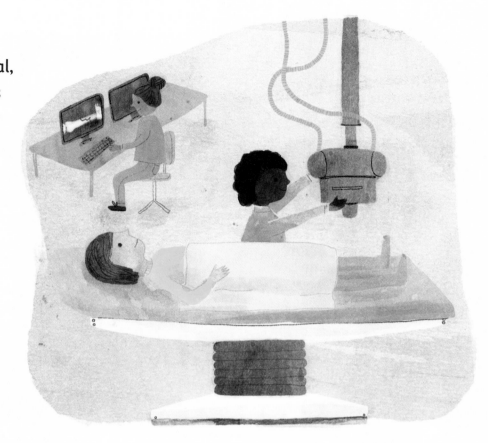

A doctor checks the X-rays and decides whether or not a patient needs a plaster cast. This is a type of wet bandage that is wrapped around a broken bone. It hardens as it dries and protects the bone while it heals.

All night the hospital is humming with activity. The lights are on, and inside, the clean hallways are busy with nurses, doctors, hospital attendants, and cleaners. Doctors do their rounds, checking on patients and making sure everyone is seen as quickly as possible.

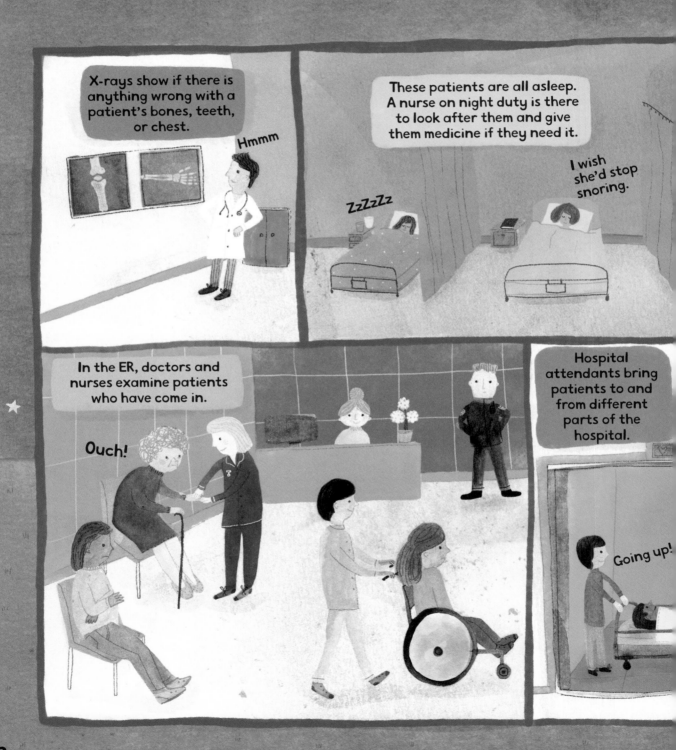

There is a special area in most hospitals called the maternity ward. This is where a woman goes to have her baby. It's very common for babies to be born in the middle of the night. People work here day and night to make sure mothers and their babies are well taken care of.

A receptionist takes urgent calls and lets patients know where to go. She calls a midwife or other nurse who is trained to look after a woman when her baby is about to be born. It can take several hours for a baby to come, and so the midwife checks the mom's pulse and takes her temperature. After that, everyone has to wait!

When the baby is close to being born, the doctor or midwife feels the mom's tummy—often the baby inside is wiggling around! Next, the baby's heartbeat is checked on a machine that makes a BIP BIP . . . BIP BIP . . . BIP BIP . . . sound. The monitor shows that the baby is well and is on its way.

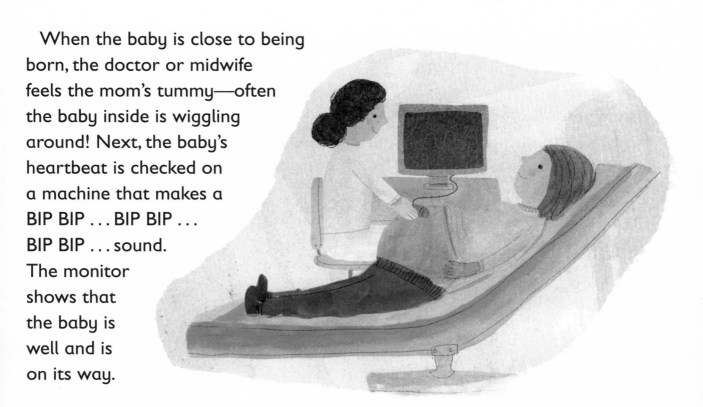

Sometimes, twins or triplets are born. Then the pediatrician—a doctor who specializes in children—checks the babies' breathing and reflexes to make sure they are healthy. A hospital assistant is on hand to bring a snack to the new mother.

The hospital doesn't stop, not even for a minute. In the morning, families come in to visit their newest additions!

Find it, Fix it!

Deep down, under the ground you walk on, pipes and tunnels run for hundreds of miles. Clean water gushes through some of them, and others carry waste away from our homes. The waste is all the stuff that you pour down the drain and flush down the toilet. These pipes and tunnels are called sewers. They can be stinky, but sewers are an incredible invention because they help keep our towns and cities clean and free from disease.

The engineer is dressed in bright, reflective gear so she can be seen. A hard hat and rubber boots are also essential for the job.

This engineer opens a manhole cover on the ground. Inside, there's a ladder leading down to a tunnel.

This engineer climbs down the rungs of the ladder. A light on his helmet will illuminate the dark.

The sound of dripping water echoes around the tunnel.

Animals make their homes in sewers, too. Rats are amazing swimmers. They also have super-sharp claws to climb pipes, and their teeth are strong enough to gnaw through concrete!

Late at night, the sewers are quiet. Most people aren't taking baths or showers, or washing clothes or dishes. With less water sloshing around, it's the perfect time for drainage engineers to go underground and inspect the sewage tunnels.

Some tunnels are very small. Others are big enough for the engineers to walk through. In big cities, engineers attach a camera to a raft or to a little robot on wheels, which can travel along the sewer. The engineers inspect the pictures on their computers to make sure that everything is flowing along nicely.

A sewer-inspection robot uses a camera to check tunnels and walls for cracks and leaks.

Sewers are hot and dark. Some of the tunnels are small and cramped.

Slippery steps go down 30 feet (10m) to more than 130 feet (40m). Some tunnels are more than 950 feet (290m) deep!

Sometimes eels, and even crabs, swim, slither, and crawl into drains and sewers.

Above the ground, things are fixed during the night, too. Cars, vans, buses, and trucks drive on roads and highways all over our cities, towns, and countryside. All those turning wheels cause a lot of wear and tear. Sometimes pot holes form in the middle of the road—or even super-sized holes called sink holes. And they need to be filled! Painted lines on highways fade over time, so they need to be brightened with fresh paint.

Some of the repairs happen during the day, but a lot of them happen at night when there is less traffic on the roads. Workers dressed in bright, reflective clothing and hard hats with lights dazzle against the darkness as they fix and mend everything in time for the morning traffic.

Away from the roads, miles of train tracks criss-cross the land. Trains carry people, and packages, and all sorts of heavy products. They speed past hedges and houses, through tunnels and over bridges.

Sometimes railroads must be closed so that train tracks can be fixed. Before work begins, it's important to put up signs and flashing lights to warn people that repairs are happening. Then, railroad workers can begin their night shift. They get to work, lifting damaged train tracks, then laying new ones. The electric signals need to be in good working order, too, so drivers know when to stop and when to go. By the time everyone is waking up, the workers and engineers are just about ready for bed!

The Rush to Market

When you wake up in the morning and see a carton of milk on the table, do you ever wonder where it came from? Maybe your parents bought it at the grocery store. But how did it get there? It's mainly thanks to the farmers who produce our food and truck drivers who transport it, traveling through the night so it arrives fresh in the morning.

Dairy farmers raise cows for their milk, and like most farmers, they wake up very early. A dairy farmer milks the cows at around 5 a.m., when many people are still fast asleep. Milking cows is a very noisy business, and there's a lot of mooing. Afterwards, it's breakfast time for the cows. They're quieter now!

The milk is collected in a truck called a tanker, and the driver transports it to a dairy factory. The next day, the rich, creamy milk is pasteurized—a process that kills germs. Then, it is poured into cartons. Another truck driver takes the milk in a refrigerated truck and delivers it to a big warehouse or directly to grocery stores.

At the grocery store, trucks come and go starting early in the morning, sometimes when it's still dark outside. They arrive with fresh milk, fruit, vegetables, meat, and fish from all over the world.

Workers take the food delivery and pass it to shelvers. The shelvers make sure that when the store is open in the morning and shoppers arrive, the shelves are full of goodies, including fresh cartons of milk!

Outside towns and cities, farmers aren't the only people busy before sunrise. Fishers are out at sea for days, working in shifts all through the day and night. They come into port with their catch early in the morning. The fish are lifted off the boat in big nets, and pots of lobsters and crabs are unloaded. Fish scales glisten, crab claws click, and seabirds swoop in from overhead, hoping to snatch a tasty snack.

The fish are quickly packed with ice to keep them cold and fresh, then they are loaded into a van. It's a rush to market so the fish can be sold!

Wholesale markets in towns and cities are also busy and open for business well before the Sun rises. Fishmongers, greengrocers, and butchers come to buy fresh fish, fruit and vegetables, and meat for their stores. The people who buy food for fancy hotels and trendy restaurants come, too—everyone is looking for the best ingredients.

Fresh flowers have been flown in overnight from flower farms all over the world. Florists come to the market to find the most beautiful blooms. They're looking for bright colors, fresh petals, and wonderful smells!

Bakers work during the night hours, too. They prepare warm, fresh loaves in time for the morning. Bakers get up after most people go to bed. The first thing they do when they arrive at the bakery is put on a special white uniform that is used in kitchens and bakeries. Bread is a very simple food—it needs only flour, water, salt, and yeast. Using those four ingredients, bakers form loaves and rolls of all shapes and sizes. The baker mixes the ingredients together to make a soft dough.

Then the dough is left alone to rest. While it's resting in the warm bakery, the dough starts to puff up! The baker shapes the puffed-up dough and pops it into the oven using a special paddle with a long handle.

A bakery is a hot, steamy place, with ovens firing, dough rising, and water steaming. The steam makes bread crust nice and crispy! By the time people wake up and the bakery doors open, all the delicious breads are ready to enjoy for breakfast—or any time.

Night Hunters

Have you ever wished that you could stay awake all night? You'd wake up just as everyone else is getting ready to sleep, with only the Moon to light your way in the darkness. If you were lucky, you would hear an owl or see a bat. These are nocturnal creatures. They sleep during the day and are active at night. They have one very good reason for choosing this topsy-turvy lifestyle . . . survival!

Some nocturnal animals, such as geckos, sleep during the day to escape the heat of the Sun. Others, such as mice, quietly creep at night to avoid being seen and eaten. But these little critters are not entirely safe. They share the darkness with creatures who are out and about precisely because they are. Meet the night hunters!

Owls are expert night hunters. They are made for it, from head to toe. Let's start with the head. Some owls have ear tufts—long feathers on top of their heads. But they have nothing to do with hearing. Scientists think owls use the tufts to communicate their mood to other owls.

An owl's ears are actually slits on either side of its head. They are hidden under lots of feathers. Some owls have one ear higher than the other, which helps them pinpoint exactly where tiny sounds are coming from. Their hearing is so good that owls can hunt in complete darkness. They can even hear a mouse when it's hiding underground.

Now let's check out their huge eyes—they are specially designed to see in the dark. Unlike most birds, who have an eye on either side of their heads, owls' eyes are on the front of their faces.

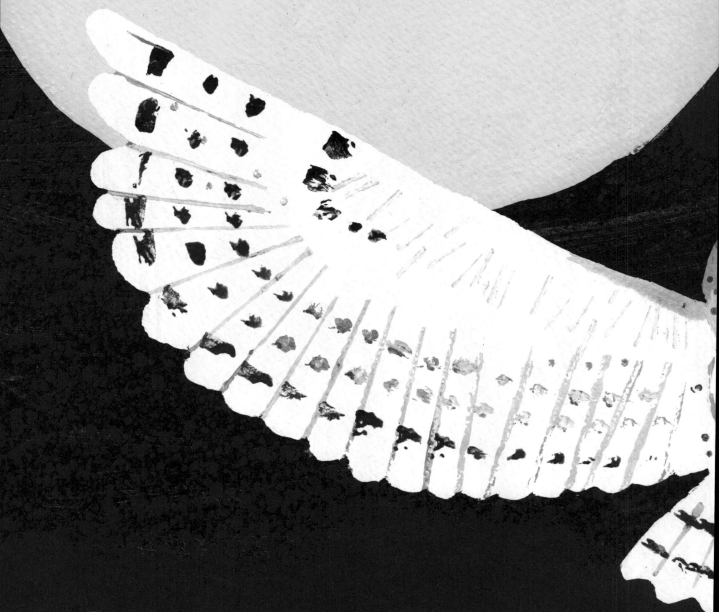

This makes them much better at figuring out how far away something is or how fast it's moving. Owls can't swivel their eyes around like humans can—they have to move their whole head to look left or right. But that's not a problem for an owl. They have 14 bones in their necks (we have only seven), which means they can turn their heads almost all the way around. It's really hard to sneak up on an owl.

But watch out . . . owls can sneak up on you! Their wings have special feathers that make them almost silent as they fly. This makes it easy for them to hear their prey but hard for their prey to hear them. And because their feathers are colored to blend in with their surroundings, owls are also really hard to see.

We've gone from head to wings. Now let's finish with toes. Owls have four creature-catching talons on each foot, which they use to crush then stab their dinner before swallowing it fur, bones, and all.
And if that's not gross enough . . .

. . . after a few hours, owls vomit up poop-like pellets containing all the bony stuff and the other parts they can't digest. Scientists sometimes open owl pellets and put the bones back together like a jigsaw puzzle. This helps them figure out which animals live in the same area as the owls.

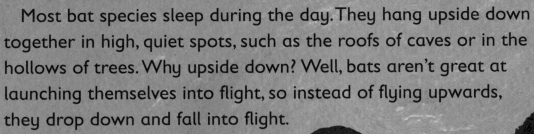

Most bat species sleep during the day. They hang upside down together in high, quiet spots, such as the roofs of caves or in the hollows of trees. Why upside down? Well, bats aren't great at launching themselves into flight, so instead of flying upwards, they drop down and fall into flight.

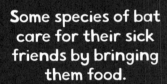

Some species of bat care for their sick friends by bringing them food.

Like other nocturnal creatures, most bats come to life at night. They have an amazing system for finding their way around in the dark. It's called echolocation, and this is how it works.

As they fly, bats let out an extremely high-pitched sound—so high that you or I can't hear it. The sound travels very quickly through the air and when it hits an object (hopefully, a tasty insect), it bounces straight back to the bats' super-sensitive ears. This lets bats know how big and how far away the object is. And if the object is moving, the bats know exactly where it's going, making them extremely efficient moth-catchers. In fact, bats are great at pest control. They can eat 2,000 juicy bugs in one night

Some bats like to hang out together and stay safe and warm in colonies.

Bats are the only mammals that can fly.

Deep in the forests of Southeast Asia lives the strangest nocturnal creature of them all. It has huge, bulging eyes and ears like a bat. Its fingers are long and skinny, and its toes have knobbly tips. Its back legs are unbelievably long—oh, and it has a stringy tail. It weighs the same as a small carton of yogurt and fits in the palm of a grown-up's hand. It's one of the world's smallest primates and has been around for 45 million years.

It's a tarsier! Like owls and bats, tarsiers are expert night hunters. They eat only meat—no greens for them, unless it's a green grasshopper, of course. They spend their nights leaping from tree to tree searching for meals, such as lizards, frogs, and bugs. Tarsiers stretch out their incredibly long legs to jump up to 30 times their own body length.

And they're good at spotting their prey—their eyeballs are huge. In fact, each of a tarsier's eyeballs weighs more than its brain, and they are specially adapted to see in the dark. Because its eyes are so big, the tarsier can't move them around. Instead it swivels its whole head, like an owl.

Scientists recently discovered that this tiny animal is the only primate that communicates solely by ultrasound—really high sounds, which we cannot hear. Scientists think tarsiers use ultrasound to tell each other where food is and alert others to danger. It also comes in handy when listening for prey. Why? A tarsier's prey also squeaks in ultrasound. So, if you're a small and tasty creature, perhaps you shouldn't go out . . . there might be a night hunter about!

The Great Sleep Escape

In the desert, the Sun can be so hot that it burns the ground. No animal wants sizzled toes—or a burnt belly, if you happen to be a snake. So it makes sense to spend the day holed up in a burrow and come out at night when it is cooler. But without the Sun, it's also much darker. This is how some clever creatures have adapted to survive living in the world's most extreme climates . . . in the dark!

This funny little rodent looks like a mishmash of lots of different creatures. It has the body of a mouse, the ears of a rabbit, the snout of a pig, and it hops around like a kangaroo! It lives in the deserts of northwest China and southern Mongolia and is so shy that it had never been filmed in the wild until just recently. It's called the long-eared jerboa, and it's the size and weight of a baked potato.

Now, let's look at those crazy ears! They are one-third bigger than the jerboa's head. As you would expect, their ears allow for excellent hearing in the dark. Jerboas can listen for rustling insects to eat and for predators who might want to eat them.

Jerboas have really short front legs, perfect for digging burrows and holding food close to their mouths. Their back legs are also pretty short. But their feet? They are extremely long and super springy. The jerboa can jump up to 6 feet (2m)—that's as high as a tall human. It uses this amazing ability to catch flying insects.

Its huge ears also release heat, which helps the jerboa cool down during the day.

This bizarre creature looks like a dinosaur, but it's actually a mammal! The pangolin is about the size of a large pet cat and lives in the tropical forests, dry woodlands, and savannahs of Asia and Africa.

A pangolin's tongue is coated with a gummy mucus, making it easy to lick up bugs.

It sleeps in burrows by day and comes out at night to hunt for termites and ants, which it sniffs out with its sensitive snout. The pangolin smashes open the termite mounds and ant hills with its strong claws, then it uses its long, sticky tongue to lick up the insects. And that tongue is *really* long—longer than its body and head combined! It can lick up 20,000 bugs in one sitting, closing off its ears and nose to stop the bugs from crawling inside.

These wonderful creatures may become extinct if we don't look out for them.

Since a pangolin doesn't have any teeth, it can't chew, so it swallows small stones to help grind up the bugs in its stomach.

Not many creatures would want to eat a pangolin. Who could chomp through all those bony scales? And pangolins have a particularly effective way of defending themselves. They simply roll into a ball and fart a foul smell from special glands near their bottom. Whoa!

What is the size of a teacup, has eight eyes and eight legs, a hairy body, and shoots sharp, pointy hairs from its tummy if threatened? It's the terrifyingly terrific tarantula!

Tarantulas have been on Earth for at least 150 million years, and there are hundreds of different species. You can find them (if you really want to) in most of the world's tropical, subtropical, and very dry regions. Even though they are the biggest spider of them all and they bite, their venom is milder than a bee sting and isn't usually harmful to humans. Tarantulas use their venom to stun their prey before biting and crushing the prey with their large jaws. Then tarantulas inject their dinner with a special chemical that turns it into a slushy juice before gulping it down. Nice!

Tarantulas are mostly nocturnal. If it's really hot, they sleep during the day and come out at night. Unlike most spiders, tarantulas don't make webs to live in. Some make their homes in logs or cracks in rocks. Others dig burrows and line them with a silky web to keep the sand out. Some tarantulas set "tripwires" outside their burrows. They lay a line of web across the entrance. If something walks into it—preferably something to eat—the tarantula will be alerted.

And here's a strange fact: tarantulas don't have ears or noses. Instead, they detect smells and sounds using the hairs on their legs and feet.

The goliath bird-eating tarantula can grow as big
as a man's hand—outstretched fingers and all!

99

The sand cat is possibly the cutest nocturnal creature found in the desert regions of Africa and Asia. Even the adults look like adorable kittens, with their large heads, and big eyes and ears. But don't be fooled by their cuteness. These cats are wild and ferocious! They are perfectly adapted for living in dry desert plains, where temperatures are sizzling hot during the day and freezing cold at night.

Sand cats are one of the only cat species to live in the desert. They are a pale, sandy color with dark stripes on their legs and tail, which makes them very difficult to see in their desert environment. The thick, dark hair on their feet protects them from the burning (or freezing) sand and helps them grip the shifting surface. They are expert diggers and use their strong feet to make burrows in the sandy soil, where they sleep during the unbearable heat of the day. When night falls and the temperature cools, sand cats leave their burrows to hunt for food.

From the outside, their ears look very similar to a pet cat. But the insides of a sand cat's ears are much bigger, giving them really good hearing!

Their fur keeps them warm as they prowl, listening for any sign of movement under the sand. When they hear a noise, they pounce, digging fast to catch their dinner—which is usually a gerbil or jerboa. They give their prey a few hard whacks with their strong paws before biting it very, very hard. Sand cats also eat insects, reptiles, and even very poisonous snakes. And these cats can go for weeks without drinking water. They get all the water they need from their food. So, whether it's hot or cold, sand cats seem to have this survival thing solved!

Watery Beds

Everyone needs a bit of shut-eye, but when your goal is not to get attacked or eaten, how do you sleep and stay alert at the same time? Most animals who live underwater have to sleep, but they can't close their eyes, and they don't have beds to lie down in. So how do they do it? Let's take a look.

The great white shark is always on the move. It has to be, because like most sharks it needs to keep water flowing over and through its body. If it stopped moving forward, it would die. So how does it rest? This question puzzled scientists for a very long time. But recently they managed to film a sleeping great white for the very first time.

The scientists used a special robot camera to follow a great white shark, which they named Emma, as she swam around Guadalupe Island in Mexico. As night fell, Emma moved closer to shore, where shallow water flowed strong and fast. She then opened her enormous jaws full of huge teeth, and started swimming against the flow—which is a bit like walking into a strong wind, but wetter. This allowed the water to flow through Emma's body without her having to use much energy to swim. The scientists could see that Emma was in a trance, like a deep daydream. They think that this is what sharks look like when they sleep. How jawsome!

The peculiar parrotfish has an unusual sleeping arrangement. After a day of pecking at coral with its beak—which is actually lots of small teeth packed closely together—it heads for bed. It tucks itself into a small rock crevice then smothers its whole body with a gooey mucus, which it spits out from its mouth. Scientists think this slimy sleeping bag protects the parrotfish by disguising the fish's smell from the highly sensitive nostrils of tiny parasites or predators who want to eat it.

The blubbery walrus has no problem floating off to sleep. Although this massive mammal sometimes snoozes under the sea, it can hold its breath for only about five minutes before it has to come up for air. If it needs a longer snooze, the walrus uses special airbags in its throat, which it fills with air—just like a balloon. This allows it to float with its head above water while taking a nap.

Walruses have been known to hang out on ice floes by hooking their long tusks over the ice and sleeping with just their noses poking out. Walruses also sleep on land, lumped together in large, lazy groups. They sleep for up to 19 hours before swimming off to sea in search of crunchy, munchy molluscs to eat.

Some walruses grip the ice as they slip off to sleep.

Did you know that dolphins and whales can drown? It may seem strange since they spend their entire lives at sea. But these marine mammals need to breathe air just as we do. Instead of breathing through their mouth or nose, they use a special nostril on top of their head called a blowhole. Dolphins and whales come up to the surface of the water and blow old air out of the hole before sucking in fresh air. Then the blowhole tightly shuts so they don't get water in their lungs and drown.

But unlike humans, dolphins and whales have to stay alert and think before they breathe, or they may accidentally suck in water instead of air.

Dolphins float like logs at the water's surface as they sleep.

So how do they rest? Well, they let only half of their brain go to sleep. The other half stays awake so that they can breathe and be aware of danger at the same time. And these clever creatures close only one eye at a time when they sleep, swapping sides every two hours for a total of eight hours.

Sometimes, dolphins float near the surface of the water without moving much as they sleep, which allows them to breathe easily through their blowholes. This position is called "logging" because the dolphins look like floating logs.

In 2008, scientists were surprised to discover a pod of sperm whales— pod is the name for a group of whales—sleeping upright on their tails. Some were even sleeping upside down! The bus-sized whales seemed to be taking 10- to 15-minute naps without moving or breathing.

Sea otters do pretty much everything in the water—eat, hunt, mate, have babies, and even sleep! They lie on their backs and bob around in groups, holding each other's paws to stop themselves from drifting apart as they float. They also tangle themselves and their babies in seaweed to avoid being swept away by swirling sea currents.

These fuzzy creatures have the thickest fur of any mammal. They need it because, unlike most marine mammals, sea otters don't have a layer of blubbery fat to keep them warm. Their coat is also waterproof, so they stay warm and snuggly as they snooze.

Sea otters' paws aren't as furry as the rest of their bodies, which is probably why they keep them out of the chilly water while they sleep.

Sea otters have two layers of fur: a
thick, dense undercoat and a longer
topcoat. The topcoat traps air and
stops the freezing water from getting
to the otters' skin.

Their poop has its own
special name – spraints.
And it's really smelly!

How Do They Sleep?

For most of us, it's pretty obvious when and where we are going to sleep. But finding the right time and place for a snooze can be a challenge for wild animals. To stay warm and safe from predators, they have developed some very interesting ways of resting.

Did you know that birds don't use nests for sleeping? Nests are for keeping eggs and chicks safe, not for birdy bedtimes. In fact, some birds don't even make nests. So where do they sleep? Well, all sorts of places, but always somewhere safe and warm. This can be high up on the branch of a tree or on the ground in shrubs or bushes. No matter where birds choose to sleep, their process of settling for the night is called "roosting."

Ducks roost together next to water and in a long line for safety. The two ducks at each end of the line only half-sleep, keeping one eye closed and one eye open to watch for danger. The ducks in the middle close both eyes, knowing that they are being looked after. And if there is any danger, they all jump into the water!

Frigate birds nest on the Galápagos Islands. They can fly for more than ten days without stopping for a break. Like ducks and dolphins, frigate birds half-sleep, always keeping one eye open as they fly . . . well . . . almost always. By strapping a special device on the birds' heads, scientists have recently discovered that these extraordinary birds sometimes go to sleep completely. They shut both eyes for a few seconds at a time *without crashing!*

Spiders take little naps throughout the day and night. They sleep in different places depending on what type of spider they are. Some sleep in the safety of their webs. Others find a dark, quiet spot to take a snooze. But wherever they choose to rest, it's hard to tell if they're asleep. Why? Because spiders don't close their eyes. They can't. Spiders don't have eyelids.

So, the best way to tell if a spider is sleeping is by looking at its hairy body language. Some species lower their bodies to the ground and curl their legs under as they snooze. Spiders that catch their prey in webs usually hang out on their silky nets in a motionless state of sleep until something lands on it. Then they immediately spring into action and eat. After eating, the spiders go back to sleep, conserving energy until their next meal drops by.

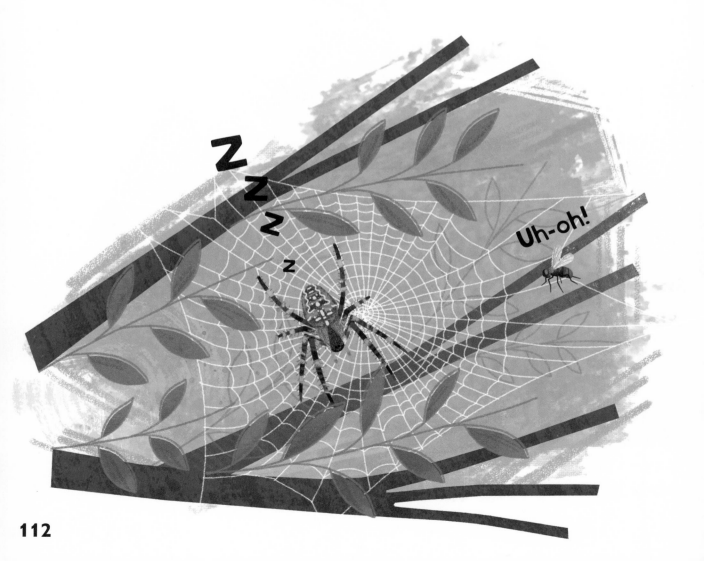

Snails are generally most active at night,
preferring warm, damp conditions so their slimy bodies
won't dry out. If it gets too cold, they retreat into their shells
to sleep, plugging the entrance with a layer of gooey mucus until it
warms up again. If conditions don't improve, snails don't care one bit. They
just sleep until the weather changes. They can stay in their shells for years
. . . yes, years! In fact, in 1846, a desert snail from Egypt that everyone
thought was dead was given to curators at the British Museum in London,
U.K. The curators then glued the snail to their display. Much to everyone's
astonishment, it woke up four years later, ate some cabbage, then lived for
another two years.

Have you ever fallen asleep on your feet? Probably not. If you did, you wouldn't be very comfortable and you would likely fall over. However, stand-up sleeping is essential for some animals to survive, because it allows them to run away at the first sign of danger. Elephants, zebras, horses, and cows are among the few animals who are specially designed to sleep this way. Here's how they fall asleep without falling over.

These animals are able to lock their legs in a straight-standing position that doesn't require much muscle effort. This allows them to doze standing up, without collapsing.

Flamingos can also sleep standing up, and they do it by balancing elegantly on just one leg. Some people can't even do that when they are awake!

For giraffes, the tallest creatures on Earth, sleeping is a real pain in the neck. Their very long necks may be great for reaching way up high for leaves to eat, but what do they do with their extreme necks when they need to rest?

In the wild, giraffes hardly ever lie down because it would take them far too long to get up, making them easy targets for predators looking for a meal. So, giraffes rest standing up, snoozing for about ten minutes at a time with their eyes barely closed in a state of half-sleep. Their necks are often tilted slightly forward as they slumber, or they may lean up against a tree or even another giraffe. They are always on the alert, with their ears twitching for any sign of danger.

On the rare occasion that they do lie down, giraffes tuck their legs under their bodies and arch their necks backwards with their heads resting on their lower backs. Imagine using your bottom as a pillow!

Sloths are one of many animals that spend their days snoozing in trees to stay safely out of reach of predators on the ground. They live in the tropical rainforests of South and Central America and come down from the trees only once a week to go to the bathroom.

In the wild, sloths sleep for about ten hours a day, securely hanging from branches by using their strong grip and very long claws.

And when they're awake, sloths just hang out, not doing much at all. Staying still makes them hard to spot in the trees. Their special fur attracts algae, a living organism, which turns the sloths green, making them even harder to see!

Another equally cute creature that lives its life in slow motion is the koala from eastern Australia. Koalas eat mostly leaves, and their favorite are from eucalyptus trees. They eat more than 2 pounds (1kg) of leaves a day—that's about the same weight as three cans of beans. Eating this much eucalyptus would be poisonous to us, but koalas have a special stomach that can handle all the poisonous stuff. All that eating and digesting takes up a lot of energy, which is why koalas spend about 18 hours a day sleeping.

As you can see, animals have some rather unusual sleeping habits. I expect you might too if you always had to keep an eye out for danger or wait for your dinner to turn up.

A Grizzly Bear's Winter

Sometimes, it's just too cold to be outside. When the days are short and food is scarce, who can blame a bear for turning its furry back on winter and hunkering down for a good, long rest?

Most grizzly bears live in Alaska and western Canada, at the very top of North America, where winters are long and cold. Here, as well as grizzlies, you will also find polar bears, black bears, brown bears, and Kodiak bears. Can you spot them on the map?

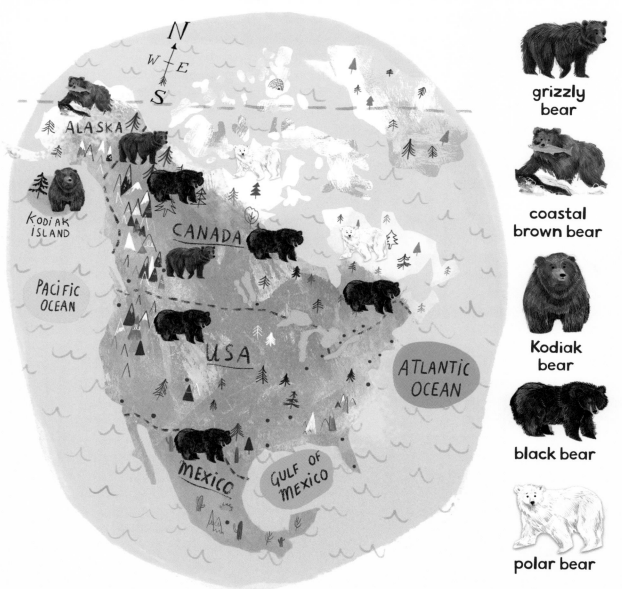

grizzly bear

coastal brown bear

Kodiak bear

black bear

polar bear

"Grizzly" means gray. That's strange, isn't it? Because grizzlies are actually a type of *brown* bear. But if you look closely, you can see that a grizzly's fur has grayish tips. This furry coat grows longer and shaggier in the winter and keeps grizzlies warm and dry during the chilly months.

Grizzly bears have an amazing sense of smell and can sniff out a meal from more than 1 mile (1.6km) away. They are omnivores, which means they eat anything nutritious that they can find, from berries, roots, and pine nuts to deer, mice, and worms. When fall comes, their appetite gets twice as big, and they simply can't get enough to eat. This extreme eating is called hyperphagia.

Oh dear, they like eating deer.

Bears love berries, too. Yum, yummy yum!

Rodents are also on the menu. Eek!

During this stage, bears never feel full and eat more than 88 pounds (40kg) of food every day. That's about the same weight as 300 blueberry muffins (depending on the size of the muffins, of course)! As a result, they can double their body weight. And they need to. The fat stored in their bodies will help them survive without food and water for several months while they sleep the winter away.

Chomp!
Chomp!

Bears stay outside for as long as there is food around. But once the cold sets in and their dinner disappears under a blanket of snow, they head for the warmth and safety of their dens. Some grizzlies start searching for a den as early as summertime.

A tree with a hole in it makes an ideal bear bedroom.

Openings in the roots of trees provide excellent winter hideaways.

Some dens have been used for hundreds of years by the same family of bears. Imagine sleeping in the same bed that your great-great-great-grandparents used!

Holes in rock crevices and caves make perfect bear bunkers!

A hollow log is a great shelter for a sleepy bear.

Other grizzly bears prefer to make their own homes for the winter. Their big feet and curved claws are excellent digging tools. And dig they do! For three to seven days they hollow out a burrow for themselves, shifting more than 1,900 pounds (860kg) of soil in the process. That's about the same weight as a small car.

A bear's den has an entrance with a sloping tunnel that leads to a cozy burrow.

Dig, dig, dig!

Bears like to dig their dens into slopes that face the wind. When winter comes, the wind blows a pile of snow across the entrance, just like a door.

In November, a bear heads for its den and rolls into a furry ball. Its breathing slows down, and its heart rate drops from about 55 beats to just 9 beats a minute. As its body gets colder, it enters a deep sleep called torpor. If it's left undisturbed, the bear won't wake for months. It won't eat, drink, or go to the bathroom because it has an amazing ability to hold it all in. How? The bear develops a plug in its bottom made from dried poop!

A Bear's Year

Jan	Feb	Mar	Apr	May	Jun	Jul	Aug	Sep	Oct	Nov	Dec

Sleeps

Wakes

Eats and eats then sleeps . . .

Although a female bear mates in early summer, her babies won't grow in her womb until she has entered her sleepy torpor. After two months, she gives birth to as many as four blind, bald, and toothless cubs. Each cub weighs no more than a large potato. They use all their baby strength to drink milk from their mother, who rarely wakes up through the whole process.

Over the next few months, the little cubs quickly grow strong from their mother's milk. When winter melts away and spring arrives, they will be ready to leave the den with their mother. Mom will be a lot thinner but fit, strong, and ready for breakfast!

Remarkable Hibernators

When winter comes, we pull on thick coats and woolly socks. We eat warm meals and drink hot chocolate by the fire. But animals can't do these things. So, what do they do when it's freezing cold and there's nothing left to eat? They find a safe place to rest until spring returns and there is food to eat once again. This rest is called hibernation, and some animals have rather surprising ways of doing it.

Ladybugs hibernate in groups under tree bark or tucked away inside leaves. Some people call this snug-as-a-bug gathering a "loveliness of ladybugs."

By the time winter arrives, only the queen bumblebee is alive. She digs a hole in the ground and hibernates all by herself until spring arrives. Then she buzzes off to find a nest to lay her eggs in.

During warmer months, the painted turtles of North America pop their heads above the water to take a breath. But what do they do in the winter when the water has a lid of ice over it and they can't come up for air? They have an amazing way of hibernating underwater: breathing air with their bottoms.

Turtles hibernate on the pond floor, where it is warmer than at the surface. And instead of breathing through their nostrils and mouth, they take in oxygen from the water through their skin and across their cloaca, which is another word for their butt.

Buried beneath the winter snow that covers forests across North America, there are frozen frogs. They are wood frogs, and if you touched one, it would feel like a frog-shaped ice cube. If you searched for a heartbeat, you wouldn't find one. Its blood would actually be frozen, too. In fact, this little amphibian would appear to be completely dead. But even though the frog is icy and statue still, it isn't dead, it's hibernating.

How does this happen? As winter approaches, wood frogs hop inside logs or shuffle under a pile of leaves. This gives them a little bit of protection as they enter hibernation, but it's not enough to stop them slowly icing over and turning into frogsicles!

As soon as the first snow touches the frog, its body releases a special sugar that protects its insides from the cold. Then more than half of the frog's body freezes—enough to stop its heart from beating and its blood from flowing.

It stays frozen for two or three months. When spring arrives, its froggy heart starts beating again and its breathing returns. The defrosted frog immediately hops off to find a mate!

The West African lungfish is a strange, eel-like creature that breathes air, walks with its fins, and lives both on land and in water. The species has survived for more than three million years!

Lungfish estivate, which is a bit like hibernation. In estivation, however, animals sleep to avoid the *heat* rather than the cold. During the dry season, the lakes where the lungfish live shrink and become muddy puddles. The floundering lungfish chew down through the mud, then wriggle around to make a burrow. They sleep with their noses pointing up into a small air hole at the top.

As the Sun shines, the mud heats up and becomes crusty. Then, lungfish do something really amazing. They stop themselves from drying up by oozing a slimy mucus from their skin, which then hardens, protecting them from the heat. They can survive like this for up to five years—without having a single poop!

When the wet season arrives and rain refills their lakes, these snotty snoozers slither back to life and swim away in search of a tasty tadpole.

Some mammals hibernate, too. Groundhogs are expert diggers. When the winter becomes too harsh, they head off to their elaborate burrows, which have a special hibernation section. It contains a bedroom, with a grass bed and a separate bathroom. It even has a few spare rooms! We don't know why groundhogs build these extra rooms—maybe they like a choice of places to sleep. Lodgers such as skunks and garter snakes sometimes move into the empty rooms.

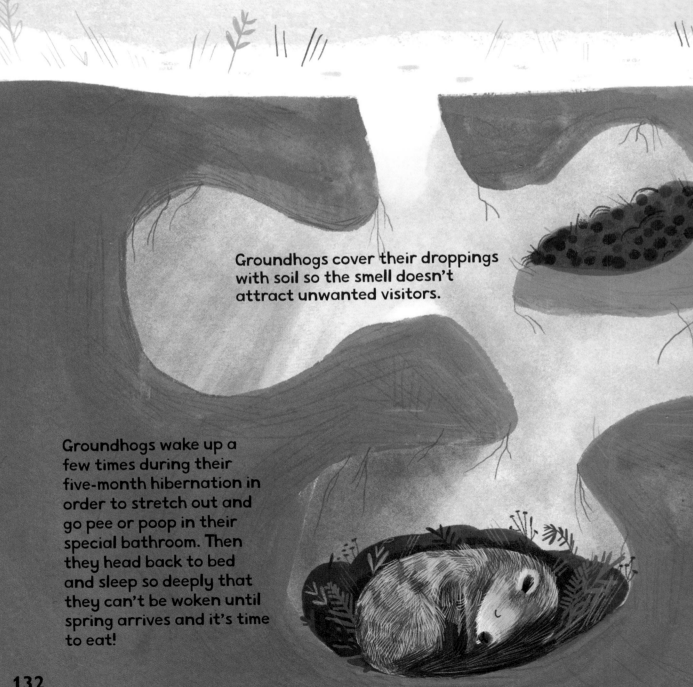

Groundhogs cover their droppings with soil so the smell doesn't attract unwanted visitors.

Groundhogs wake up a few times during their five-month hibernation in order to stretch out and go pee or poop in their special bathroom. Then they head back to bed and sleep so deeply that they can't be woken until spring arrives and it's time to eat!

Like bears, groundhogs fill up on food before their long winter rest and use their body fat to stay alive. As they sleep, their heart rate slows to only five beats a minute and their temperature drops to 41°F (5°C)—that's about as cold as the inside of a fridge. Ch-ch-chilly, but what a very cool way to spend the winter months!

Groundhog burrows have multiple exits so the animals can escape if they need to.

A bundle of garter snakes takes advantage of a spare room.

Sunrise to Sunset

Look out your window and watch the world. Watch a squirrel climb a tree and a ladybug crawl across a leaf. Watch how the sky changes as the Sun rises in the morning then drops down at sunset, before darkness falls.

From here on Earth, it looks like the Sun is moving, but it's not. We are moving—you, me, and the planet we live on.

Earth rotates—or spins—on an axis. The axis is an invisible line that our planet rotates around, like the center of a spinning top. It takes 24 hours for the Earth to complete a single spin. That's why a day is 24 hours long.

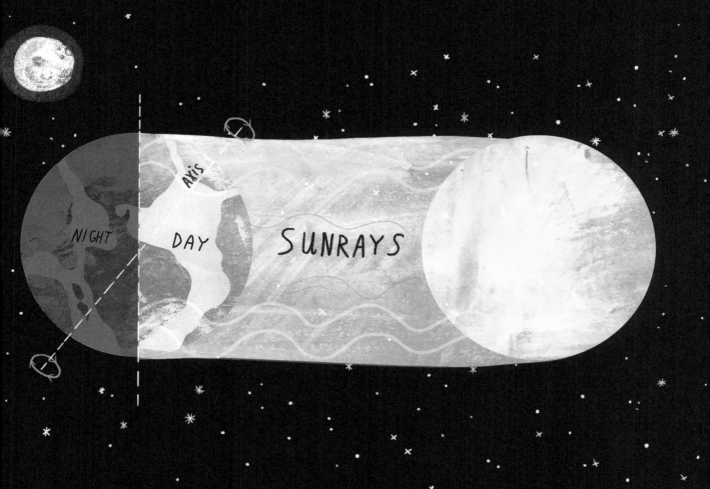

While the Earth is spinning, the Sun stays in the same spot. Sometimes the side of the planet we are on faces the Sun, and the Sun's light shines on us. This is daytime. At other times the side of the planet we are on faces away from the Sun. This is nighttime.

When it's night on your side of Earth, on the other side of the planet it's day. And when it is day on your side, the other side is in darkness. So while kids are waking up in Colorado, it's bedtime in India.

Because of the way Earth rotates, the Sun always appears to rise in the east and set in the west. You can tell if the Sun is high or low in the sky by looking at your shadow. When the Sun is high, your shadow will be puddled around your feet. When the Sun is low, your shadow stretches across the ground.

At sunrise and sunset, the
sunlight looks like a melted
popsicle. Delicious!

The Earth spins, and the Sun starts to disappear below the horizon.
Sometimes the sky changes color—red, orange, gold, pink. That's because
of the way light is scattered through the air.

Once the Sun goes down, for a short while it's twilight, the time
between sunset and night. Then it gets dark, and we can see the Moon
and stars speckle the sky, unless clouds get in the way.

As it gets dark, if you watch carefully, you'll notice things changing. Many flowers close up their petals to protect their insides from the cold. Animals that we rarely see during the day venture out. Like owls and other night hunters, these animals are nocturnal, which means they are active at night. On summer nights, fireflies come out, looking for love. They light up like tiny flashlights to impress a possible mate.

Fireflies light up their bottoms!

Some pets are nocturnal, too. That's why hamsters run wildly in their exercise wheel when you're trying to sleep.

The Earth spins. Night becomes dawn, and nocturnal animals return to their homes, nests, and burrows to rest. The stars disappear. The Sun rises. Flowers open again. Birds start to sing. Diurnal animals—animals that are active during the day—shake off sleep. People do, too. The Sun tells the world it's time to wake up.

The Midnight Sun

In summer, the Sun rises earlier and sets later than it does in winter. Depending on where you live, it might still be dark when you wake up in winter, and still be light outside when you go to bed in summer—just as Robert Louis Stevenson wrote in his poem, *Bed in Summer*.

"In winter I get up at night
And dress by yellow candle-light.

In summer, quite the other way,
I have to go to bed by day."

So why is the length of daylight different depending on what season it is? Just as the Earth rotates, or spins, in space, causing day and night, it also circles around—or orbits—the Sun.

Earth is at a slight tilt. When the part of the Earth that we live on is tilted toward the Sun, the days are longer and warmer. That's summer. When the part of Earth we are on is tilted away from the Sun, the days are shorter and cooler. That's winter.

EARTH'S ORBIT

SUMMER

WINTER

SUN

WINTER

SUMMER

The longest day of the year—or the day with the most hours of sunlight—is known as the summer solstice. The shortest day of the year—the day with the fewest hours of sunlight—is the winter solstice. These days fall around June 21st and December 21st each year. The tricky part? Because of Earth's tilt, December 21st is the winter solstice in the northern half of the planet, but it's the summer solstice in the southern half! That's why when it's summer in Australia, it's winter in Canada.

January in Australia   January in Canada

In countries such as Sweden, Norway, Greenland, Iceland, and Finland, summer days are really long. The Sun stays up until 11 o'clock at night, or even later. In some places that are even farther north, such as northern Alaska, the Sun never drops below the horizon. It's light for 24 hours. These places are sometimes known as the "Land of the Midnight Sun."

Of course, during winter in these far northern places, it's the opposite. The Sun never rises above the horizon. It's dark all day.

Since long, long ago, people have believed the solstices to be special. Around the world, they were often celebrated with feasts and festivals. In Sweden, the longest day of the year is called Midsommar. It's a national holiday. Swedes sing songs, wear flower crowns, and dance around a midsommar pole.

On the shortest day of the year, the Zuni and Hopi people of North America celebrate Soyal. They ask kachina spirits to bring back the Sun.

A festival called Dongzhi marks the winter solstice in China. People make dumplings or brightly colored rice balls to prepare for winter. In Taiwan, nine-layer cakes shaped like lucky animals, such as chickens, pigs, cows, and sheep, are left near family tombs.

In Iran, the winter solstice is a holiday called Yalda. Some people stay awake all night to welcome the morning Sun.

There's another solstice festival that many people around the world celebrate—Christmas! The date of Jesus's birth isn't listed anywhere in the Bible. Some historians think church founders decided on December 25th in part because it was close to the winter solstice, a holiday many people around the world already honored.

The Northern Lights

In the northernmost parts of northern countries, where the winters are long and winter days are short, people sometimes see a special sight: the Northern Lights. The Northern Lights are bands of colors that shift across the sky. Usually they are yellowish green, but every once in a while they are blue, violet, or pink. The Northern Lights are also known as *aurora borealis*, or the northern dawn.

The Northern Lights take the shape of rays, bands, or arcs. But they can also look like arches, crowns, or curtains. The auroras happen day and night, every day of the year, but most of the time the light from the Sun prevents people from seeing them. The best time to see the Northern Lights is on a clear night during late fall, in winter, or in early spring. People plan special trips just to watch the Northern Lights. They travel to Alaska, Greenland, Iceland, or the northern parts of Russia, Norway, Sweden, and Finland. They may sleep outside in a tent to watch the sky.

What causes the Northern Lights? The Sun! Storms on the Sun create solar wind, which carries energy through space and to Earth. Then Earth's poles act like magnets pulling particles from the solar wind toward them. These particles smash into the gases in Earth's atmosphere, letting energy out as light—the Northern Lights and the Southern Lights.

That's right. The South Pole has its own light display, the Southern Lights or *aurora australis*. These lights happen at the same time as the ones up north. They mirror each other.

Some people claim they have heard the Northern Lights. They say the sky swishes or crackles with the shifting lights. But how these auroras make noise is a mystery.

THE NORTHERN LIGHTS

THE SOUTHERN LIGHTS

Earth isn't the only planet to have auroras. Jupiter, Saturn, Uranus, and Neptune have them, too. Thanks to the Sun, the Earth and other planets in our solar system have beautiful light shows in the night sky.

A Trip to the Stars

The night sky is filled with stars. From here on Earth, they all look similar—tiny, white, and twinkly. But imagine flying into space to see the stars up close. Out there, it's obvious how different stars are! The first star we'd arrive at is the Sun. Yes, the Sun is a star, and a pretty

ordinary one. It's not the biggest or the smallest, the hottest or the coldest, the oldest or the youngest. It's been around for about five billion years and will probably go on for five billion more. That's a relief! We need the Sun for so many things, including light and heat.

The oldest stars are about 13 billion years old. And the youngest are younger than you. New stars are born all the time. Some scientists estimate that thousands of stars are born every second.

The Sun is the center of our solar system and the only star in it. That's unusual. Many stars come in pairs, and the stars rotate around each other or in clusters. But our Sun is a lonely star.

Even though stars look white in the night sky, they are different colors. We often relate the color blue to the cold and red to heat, but with stars it's the opposite. The hottest stars are blue and the coolest stars are red.

Our Sun is a type of star called a yellow dwarf. There are also white dwarfs, no larger than Earth, which form at the end of a star's life. Some stars are giants—or supergiants! They are hundreds of times bigger than the Sun.

BETELGEUSE

ORION'S BELT

THE
ORION NEBULA

RIGEL

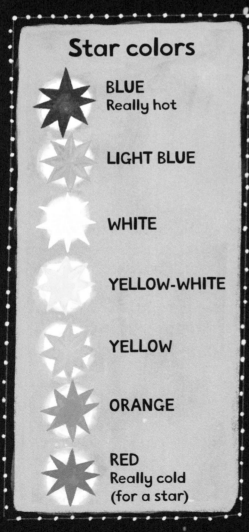

Star colors

BLUE
Really hot

LIGHT BLUE

WHITE

YELLOW-WHITE

YELLOW

ORANGE

RED
Really cold
(for a star)

A star has many layers. The center is called the core. It's like the pit in the middle of a peach but a whole lot hotter.

Twinkle, twinkle, little star? Not in space! Not only aren't stars little, but in space, they don't twinkle either. The twinkling we see at night is caused by Earth's atmosphere.

You can't walk on a star like you can on Earth because stars aren't solid. They're made of gases, just like the invisible air around us. But unlike air, these gases burn really well, which is why stars are so hot! A star is actually a huge ball of burning gas.

Just like us, stars change over time. They can grow into giant stars. Sometimes they explode and star particles get flung across the darkness. These particles go on to make new stars and planets. Exploding stars are the building blocks of the universe. Stars can also become black holes. The gravity of a black hole is so strong that it sucks in everything around it.

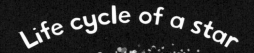

Life cycle of a star

STELLAR NEBULA

This is where stars are born.

AVERAGE STAR

MASSIVE STAR

The star gets hotter, the core gets smaller, and the rest of the star gets bigger. This is a red giant.

RED GIANT

The star grows to become a red supergiant.

RED SUPERGIANT

The outer layers of the star drift off into space. This is a planetary nebula.

PLANETARY NEBULA

The core might collapse and explode: this is a supernova!

SUPERNOVA

The star shrinks and becomes a white dwarf.

WHITE DWARF

Sometimes the core of a star survives a supernova to become a very heavy star called a neutron star. Or it might become a black hole. Nothing escapes a black hole, not even light!

NEUTRON STAR   BLACK HOLE

154

What's the next closest star to Earth after the Sun? Alpha Centauri. It's in the Milky Way galaxy—just like the Sun and the Earth. There are lots of other stars in the Milky Way, too—billions of them. And the Milky Way is just one of many galaxies in the universe.

THE MILKY WAY

EARTH

The universe contains everything that exists: all the stars, planets, moons, space, galaxies, you, me, all matter, even time. It's also constantly changing. The universe is growing. Old stars are dying. New stars are born. And except for our Sun, all the stars are very far away. They are so far away that the light from them takes years to reach Earth. The light from the Sun, on the other hand, takes eight minutes to reach our planet. We're lucky to have such a stellar star nearby!

Stargazing

Over time, we've gotten better at stargazing. Thousands, even hundreds of years ago, what people could see of space was only what they could observe with just their eyes—mainly the Sun, the Moon, a planet or two, and the stars.

But people found new ways to stargaze. One really good way was the telescope. With mirrors and curved glass lenses that focus light rays, a telescope makes faraway things appear closer. Imagine how surprised people must have been when they looked through a telescope for the first time and saw things in the sky that they had never seen before!

The first telescope was invented in the Netherlands in the early 1600s. A few years later, an Italian scientist named Galileo made his own, even better, telescope. Galileo turned his telescope to the night sky and discovered all sorts of things. He found that there were many more stars than anyone could see with just their eyes. Galileo also changed our understanding of Earth's place in the universe by discovering that our planet revolved around the Sun and was not at the center of the universe, as people believed at the time.

People didn't want to believe Galileo. What he said went against the teachings of the Roman Catholic Church. They were sure the Earth was the center of the universe. But because of the books Galileo wrote, his theories spread all over Europe, paving the way for hundreds of years of space discoveries.

Since Galileo's time, telescopes have gotten even better, and even bigger! The biggest telescopes are in observatories. An observatory is a place for studying outer space and everything in it, such as comets and planets—and stars, of course. Observatories are usually built far away from cities, because cities give off too much light from buildings and offices, from streetlights and cars. To see the stars well, it helps to be somewhere that's very dark with a very clear sky.

Some observatories are in deserts.

Some are high up on mountains.

Some are on faraway islands.

And some observatories are out in space.

Space observatories have great views but are hard to fix if something goes wrong!

If you visit an observatory, you might run in to scientists working there. Scientists who study the stars, space, and the universe are called astronomers.

Famous scientists who have added to our knowledge of the universe include Galileo, Isaac Newton, Albert Einstein, and Stephen Hawking. They haven't figured everything out. The universe still has many secrets, and astronomers are working to unlock them.

Stories in the Stars

Long ago, when people stared up at the night sky, they saw patterns in the stars. They imagined the patterns looked like things they knew, such as animals, gods, and heroes. These star patterns are called constellations. About 100 years ago, a group of scientists got together and chose 88 constellations to make official. This meant that everyone would be able

NORTHERN
HEMISPHERE

to refer to the stars in the same way. Which stars we see in the night sky depends on two things: the time of the year and which part of the Earth we are looking from. If we are in the northern half of the world, we see different stars than if we are in the southern half. The north and south halves of our planet are known as the northern and southern hemispheres.

The only constellation visible from both hemispheres is Orion.

SOUTHERN HEMISPHERE

Throughout history, people have created stories about the star patterns that they saw in the sky. The ancient Greeks named the constellations after characters from myths. Pegasus is a flying horse, Orion is a giant hunter who is raising his club and shield, and Leo is the lion that was killed by Hercules, one of the most famous ancient Greek heroes. The Greek names are still used for these constellations today.

PEGASUS

ORION

ORION'S BELT

LEO

Orion's belt is an asterism. An asterism is a pattern of stars that isn't a full constellation.

The people of southern Africa also saw animals in the stars. For example, they saw four giraffes in the group of stars known as the Southern Cross.

They saw three zebras galloping away from a hunter in the group of stars known as Orion's belt.

Also in the southern hemisphere, ancient aboriginal Australians saw the dark clouds of the Milky Way as a huge floating emu. The emu chases a possum called Bunya, who scrambles up a tree and hides for safety.

The stories in the stars have helped people make sense of the mysterious night sky and have been passed down for generations.

If you want to spot some star patterns for yourself, you can look up at the sky at any time on a clear night. Here are some tips for gazing at the stars. Remember to ask a grown-up to help you.

★ Wait until it gets dark, and move far away from lights. Give your eyes time to get used to the darkness.

★ Go up high. Sometimes tall buildings block part of the sky. The higher you are, the better your view will be.

★ Check the weather. Clear skies are good for stargazing. Don't go out on a rainy or snowy night. The clouds will get in the way.

★ Make a red flashlight. Cover the bright end of a flashlight with red tissue paper and secure it with a rubber band. It will help you see in the dark but won't mess up your night vision while looking at the stars.

- ★ Bundle up! The sky is at its best on cold, clear winter nights.
- ★ Don't stargaze if the Moon is full. The Moon gives off a lot of light, which makes it harder to see the stars. Try stargazing when the Moon is just a sliver.
- ★ Get a star map. A star map is exactly what it sounds like—a map of the stars. It can help you figure out which stars you are seeing when you look up. You can find star maps in books, you can print one out, or you can download an app on a phone—but ask a grown-up first.

I See the Moon

Have you ever glimpsed a silvery light through your curtains at night? Draw them back and you might see a full Moon. It's the brightest object in the night sky. The Moon is almost as old as planet Earth.

Earth is four times bigger than the Moon. So if you imagine our planet as a basketball, the Moon would be roughly the size of a tennis ball. The Moon was created in the early days of the solar system when the Earth was young.

Astronomers think that 4.5 billion years ago, the Earth and a planet called Theia crashed into each other . . .

BOOM!

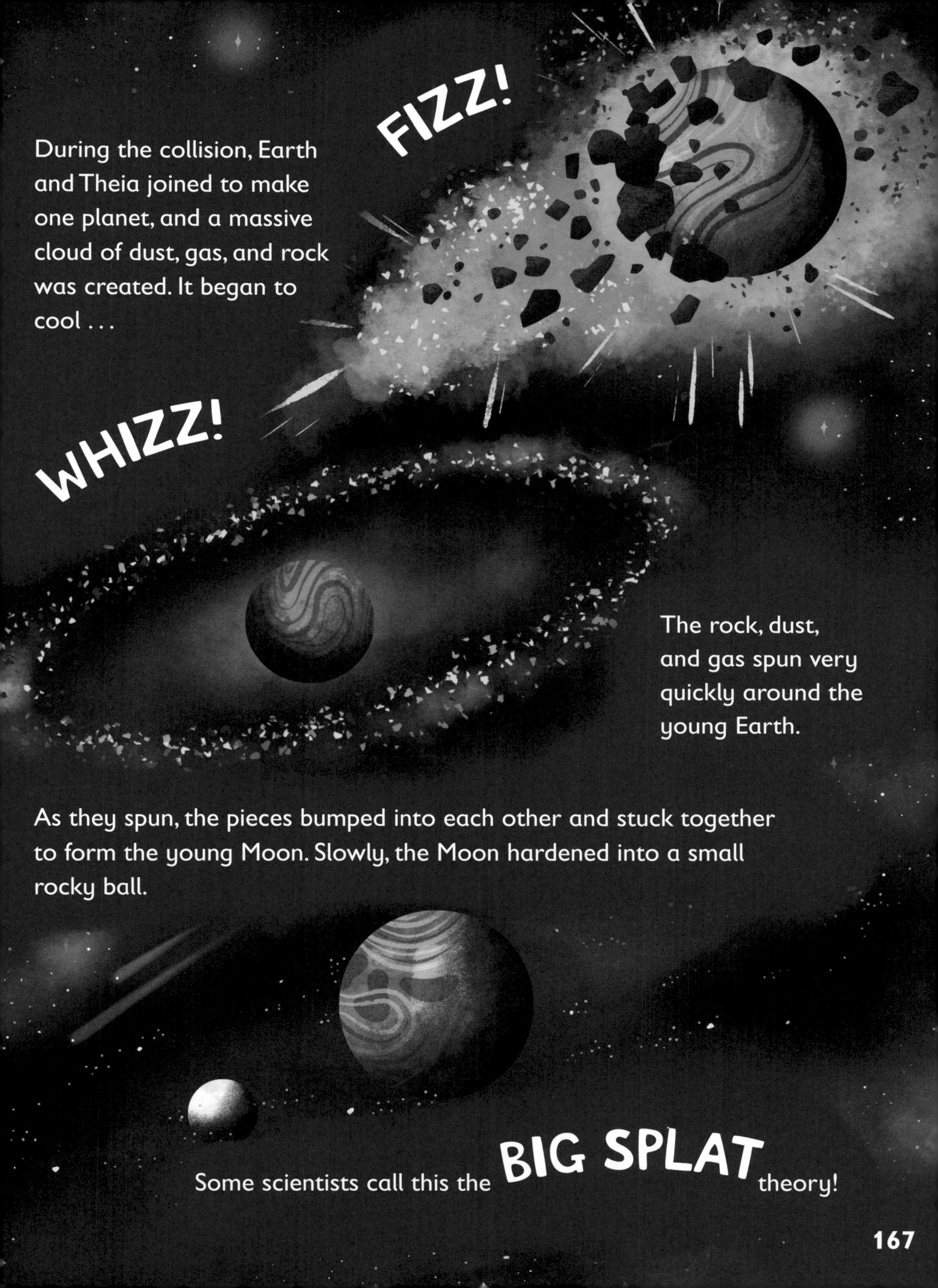

During the collision, Earth and Theia joined to make one planet, and a massive cloud of dust, gas, and rock was created. It began to cool . . .

FIZZ!

WHIZZ!

The rock, dust, and gas spun very quickly around the young Earth.

As they spun, the pieces bumped into each other and stuck together to form the young Moon. Slowly, the Moon hardened into a small rocky ball.

Some scientists call this the **BIG SPLAT** theory!

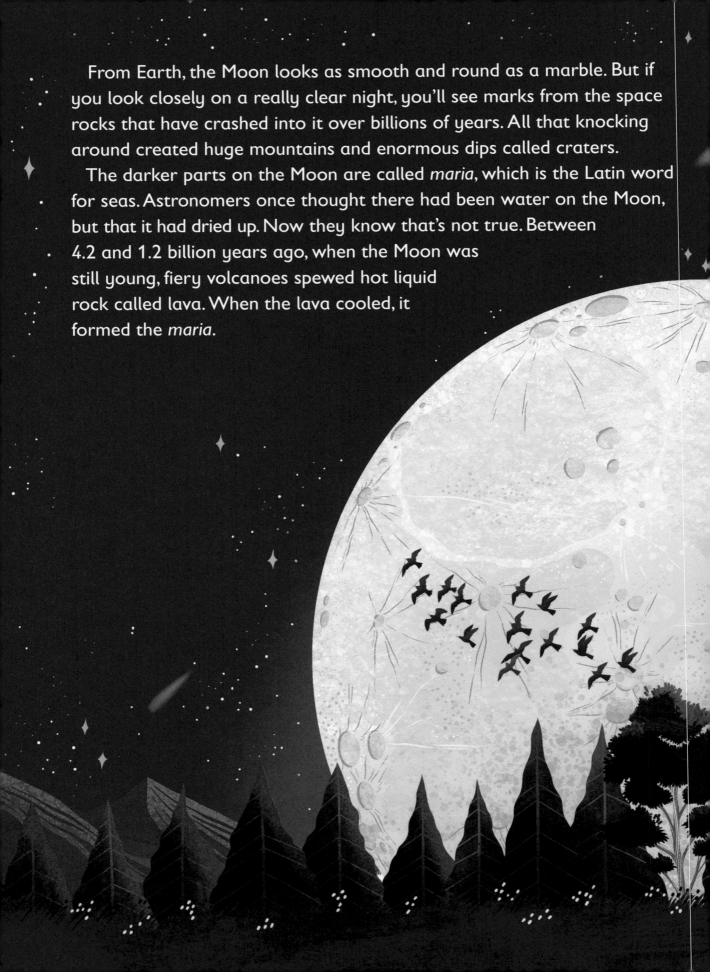

From Earth, the Moon looks as smooth and round as a marble. But if you look closely on a really clear night, you'll see marks from the space rocks that have crashed into it over billions of years. All that knocking around created huge mountains and enormous dips called craters.

The darker parts on the Moon are called *maria*, which is the Latin word for seas. Astronomers once thought there had been water on the Moon, but that it had dried up. Now they know that's not true. Between 4.2 and 1.2 billion years ago, when the Moon was still young, fiery volcanoes spewed hot liquid rock called lava. When the lava cooled, it formed the *maria*.

Besides mountains and craters, you won't find much else on the Moon. If you're looking for trees, water, or even clouds, you can forget about it. You might find a tiny amount of ancient ice in craters at the north and south poles, but not much else. Up close, this rocky ball is covered with powdery stuff called regolith, which is just plain old dust and rock.

At night, the Moon is colder than you could ever imagine. But when the Sun shines, the Moon becomes so hot it's a boiling 248°F (120°C). And there isn't any air on the Moon, which is why astronauts have to wear special suits when they're walking on the surface.

With no water, no clouds, no air, and no life, the Moon has stayed unchanged in the night sky for billions of years.

From Earth, we see only one side of the Moon. We call it the "near side" because it faces us. The side of the Moon that we never see is called the "far side." Sometimes the near side of the Moon is lit up and the far side is in darkness, and sometimes it is the other way around. The line where the light and the shadow meet is called the "terminator."

Sun

Earth

Moon

terminator

Although the Moon shines brightly in the night sky, it doesn't make its own light. What we see is sunlight reflecting off the Moon.

The Moon spins very slowly in space, taking about 27 days to make one rotation. This means one day on the Moon is 27 Earth days. As the Moon turns, it also moves around Earth on a journey called an orbit. It takes about 27 days for the Moon to complete one orbit around Earth.

Have you noticed that the Moon seems to change shape a little every day? Sometimes it looks like a silver coin. Other times, the Moon looks like a bright banana. This is really a trick of the light. As the Moon travels around the Earth, the Sun lights up different parts of it. The part of the Moon we can see changes a little every day. The shapes we see are called phases.

New Moon

Waxing crescent Moon

First quarter Moon

Waxing gibbous

Full Moon

Waning gibbous

Last quarter Moon

Waning crescent Moon

When the Sun lights up the whole far side of the Moon, the side facing us looks dark. This is a new Moon. And sometimes the Moon looks like a shiny banana. This is a crescent Moon.

A quarter Moon happens when roughly half of the side facing us is lit up, and a gibbous Moon is when more than half of it is lit up. When the Moon seems to grow bigger, it's called waxing. When it appears to grow smaller, we say it is waning.

A full Moon happens when the Sun lights up the whole side of the Moon that is facing us.

Which phase of the Moon can you see tonight?

Fly Me to the Moon

About 400 years ago, in a town called Padua in Italy, there lived a man named Galileo Galilei. He loved math and was a professor at the university in Padua. In his spare time, Galileo studied the Moon and the night sky.

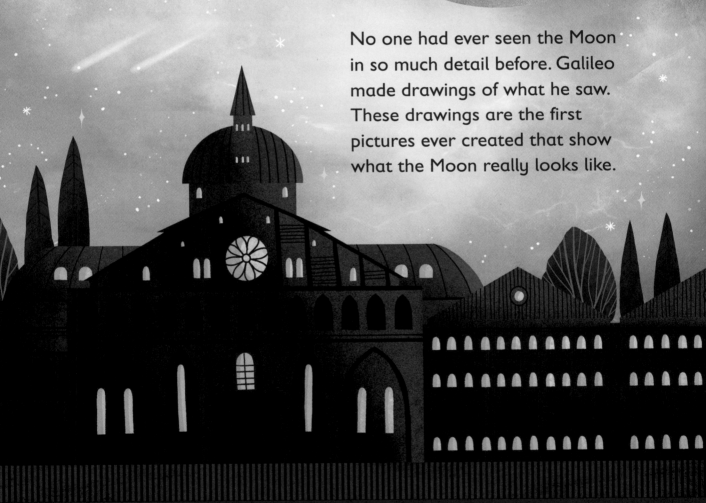

One fall evening in 1609, Galileo gazed at the Moon using a powerful telescope that he had made himself. What he saw amazed him. The Moon wasn't smooth, like most people thought; it had mountains and craters!

No one had ever seen the Moon in so much detail before. Galileo made drawings of what he saw. These drawings are the first pictures ever created that show what the Moon really looks like.

About 300 years after Galileo looked at the Moon through his telescope, a man named Robert Goddard had the idea of sending a rocket and people into space. At the time, a lot of people thought Goddard was crazy. No one had ever been to space before!

Goddard was a phenomenal inventor. He built the world's first liquid-fueled rocket, which he launched in 1926. Although this rocket didn't reach the dizzy heights of space or have people on board, it inspired other inventors.

Over the years, many rockets traveled to space, but none of them with a person on board. This changed in 1961 when Russian cosmonaut Yuri Gagarin traveled around Earth in a rocket called Vostok 1. It would take another eight years before anyone successfully landed on the Moon.

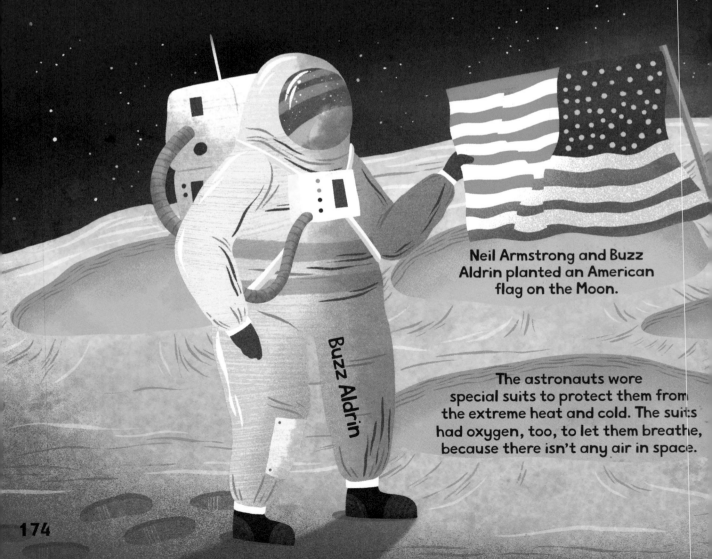

Buzz Aldrin

Neil Armstrong and Buzz Aldrin planted an American flag on the Moon.

The astronauts wore special suits to protect them from the extreme heat and cold. The suits had oxygen, too, to let them breathe, because there isn't any air in space.

In July 1969, the American space flight Apollo 11 hurtled into space with three astronauts on board: Neil Armstrong, Buzz Aldrin, and Michael Collins. Armstrong took the first ever steps on the Moon's surface, followed by Aldrin. (Collins stayed in orbit around the Moon.) So Goddard's idea about sending people to space wasn't so crazy after all.

The Eagle has landed!

Beautiful view!

Neil Armstrong

A special vehicle called a lunar module carried Armstrong and Aldrin to the surface of the Moon. The astronauts named this vehicle The Eagle.

The astronauts' boots left crisp footprints on the Moon. The footprints are still there today.

Only 12 people have walked on the Moon since that famous day in 1969. But many men and women have made the amazing journey into space. Some astronauts even live in space, in a space station. In fact, there are normally about six people on board the International Space Station. They do important experiments while orbiting the planet and send the results back to scientists on Earth.

In 2018, China sent a rocket to the far side of the Moon. It beamed back incredible photos of a huge crater, one of the largest in our whole solar system.

Moon village

Scientists hope to use 3-D printers to construct buildings using moondust.

Scientists might explore the surface of the Moon in space vehicles with huge bumpy wheels.

It won't be long before a rocket takes off to the Moon again. Scientists and astronomers already talk about the possibility of building a "Moon village." If we build a permanent structure on the Moon, scientists could conduct experiments there. But astronauts may also use it as a base to explore other planets. It would involve long journeys—flying from the Moon to Mars would take about nine months. And just imagine what life would be like for people living on the Moon . . . Who knows, maybe it would look something like this.

Once there is a permanent station, astronauts might whizz up to the Moon and back again in rockets, a bit like commuters on a train.

An enormous satellite dish could capture radio signals and take photos to beam back to Earth.

Moon Mysteries

Why are we so fascinated by the Moon? Part of its mystery is that it seems to change all the time. Sometimes it even glows red.

Sun

About twice a year, something special occurs. The Earth and the Moon line up with the Sun. When this happens, the Earth blocks the Sun's light, casting a long, dark shadow on the Moon. This event is called a lunar eclipse. During this time, the Moon takes on a fiery red glow—it's called a blood Moon.

In ancient times people looked at the Moon and thought it was amazing. They wondered where it came from and if anything lived there. When a lunar eclipse happened and they saw the Moon darken and turn red, they found it scary and wondered if something else was going to happen. They invented stories to explain this strange event, and those stories were passed down, from generation to generation.

When Earth blocks the light from the Sun,
the Moon appears to be blood red!

Moon shadows

As the Earth gradually moves between the Sun and the Moon, it casts a shadow, which slowly creeps across the face of the Moon.

Our ancestors wove these stories of the Moon into the fabric of their lives, and they are still told the world over.

In China, Chang'e is the goddess of the Moon. One story says that Chang'e's husband gave her a potion to look after. This potion would make whoever drank it live forever. One day, when her husband was away, a student of his tried to steal the potion. To stop him, Chang'e drank the potion herself. She floated all the way to the Moon, where she still lives today, watching over the world.

The Inca people of South America lived about 500 years ago. They believed in Mama Quilla, Mother Moon. The Inca thought that when a lunar eclipse happened, Mama Quilla was being attacked by a fierce creature. The Inca shook their spears and made their dogs howl at the Moon to scare the creature away.

Togo and Benin are countries in West Africa where the Batammaliba people live. They tell a story of how angry villagers fought with one another. The first two mothers, Puka Puka and Kuiyecoke, tried to stop the fighting, but the villagers wouldn't listen. The mothers darkened the Sun and the Moon and caused an eclipse. This frightened the villagers so much that they stopped fighting and made up. Today, an eclipse is seen as a time when people make peace with their family, friends, and neighbors.

Lullabies Around the World

Did you know that you could hear your mom's voice before you were born? That's right, at 24 weeks, when you were the same size as a cantaloupe, you could hear her voice soothe you as you grew in her tummy. In fact, even if a baby is deaf, it can still feel its mother's voice rumble through its tiny body.

Since ancient times, people from all over the world have calmed their babies by singing to them. What these parents knew instinctively, and what scientists have recently proven, is that singing actually slows children's heart rate down and prepares them for rest.

And the singer doesn't need to have a beautiful voice to make this magic happen. All that's required is a loving, gentle voice and a rhythmic melody to sing. Oh, and maybe a cuddle! We're never too old to be sung to, so if you're a little wound up or struggling to fall asleep, try listening to one of these lullabies from around the world.

Hush little baby

American lullaby

Hush, little baby, don't say a word,
Papa's gonna buy you a mockingbird.
And if that mockingbird don't sing,
Papa's gonna buy you a diamond ring.
And if that diamond ring is brass,
Papa's gonna buy you a looking glass.
And if that looking glass gets broke,
Papa's gonna buy you a billy goat.
And if that billy goat don't pull,
Papa's gonna buy you a cart and bull.
And if that cart and bull turn over,
Papa's gonna buy you a dog named Rover.
And if that dog named Rover don't bark,
Papa's gonna buy you a horse and cart.
And if that horse and cart turn round,
You'll still be the sweetest little babe in town,
Still be the sweetest little babe in town.

Fais dodo, Colas mon p'tit frère

French lullaby

Fais dodo, Colas mon p'tit frère
Fais dodo, t'auras du lolo
Maman est en haut
Qui fait du gâteau
Papa est en bas
Qui fait du chocolat
Fait dodo, Colas mon p'tit frère
Fait dodo, t'auras du lolo.

Go to sleep, Colas, my little brother
Go to sleep, you will have your milk
Mommy is upstairs
Making some cakes
Daddy is downstairs
Making hot chocolate
Go to sleep, Colas, my little brother
Go to sleep, you will have your milk.

Iny hono izy ravorombazaha

Malagasy lullaby

Iny hono izy ravorombazaha
Ento misidina mankany antsaha
Ento misidina ambony
Rahefa mangina avereno,
O o o o o, ooooooo.

Here's my baby, oh beautiful foreign bird,
Fly him up above the countryside,
Fly him high up in the sky,
When he's quiet, bring him back,
O o o o o, ooooooo.

Arrorró mi niño

Latin American lullaby

Arrorró mi niño,
arrorró mi sol,
arrorró pedazo
de mi corazón.

Estela niño lindo
ya quiere dormir;
háganle la cuna
de rosa y jazmín.

Hush-a-bye my baby,
Hush-a-bye my Sun,
Hush-a-bye oh piece
of my heart.

This pretty child
wants to sleep already;
make him a cradle
of rose and jasmine.

Edo komoriuta

Japanese lullaby

Nennen korori yo, Okorori yo.
Bōya wa yoi ko da, Nenne shina

Bōya no omori wa, Doko e itta?
Ano yama koete, Sato e itta.

Sato no miyage ni, Nani morotta
Denden taiko ni, Shō no fue.

Hush-a-bye, hush-a-bye now!
My good baby, sleep.

Where did my boy's babysitter go?
Beyond that mountain, back to her home.

As a souvenir from her home,
what did you get?
A toy drum and a shō flute.

Meet the Authors & Illustrators

The night sky is full of stars, and so is this book! We are very grateful to all the authors and illustrators who have brightened these pages with their illuminating stories and pictures.

AUTHORS

Jackie McCann has worked in children's publishing for many years and is an experienced writer and editor. She specializes in children's nonfiction and works with brilliant authors, illustrators, and designers to create children's novelty books. She lives in London, U.K. *Jackie's stories: "A Busy Night at the Hospital," "Find it, Fix it!," "The Rush to Market," "I See the Moon," "Fly Me to the Moon," and "Moon Mysteries."*

Jen Arena is a former Editorial Director at Random House Books for Young Readers and is now a full-time author. She has written many books for children, both fiction and nonfiction, including *Lady Liberty's Holiday, Long Tall Lincoln, Pink Snow and Other Weird Weather, Besos for Baby,* and *Marta! Big and Small.* She lives in Tampa, Florida. *Jen's stories: "Sunrise to Sunset," "The Midnight Sun," "The Northern Lights," "A Trip to the Stars," "Stargazing," and "Stories in the Stars."*

Rachel Valentine is the author of several children's picture books, including the *Marmaduke* series. She lives and works in Kent, U.K., with her family and her dog, Scout. *Rachel's stories: "Why Do We Sleep?," "What are Dreams?," "Heading to Bed," "King Tut's Beds," "Beds Around the World," "Warm as Toast!," "Asleep in Space," "Rock-a-bye Sleeping," and "Sleeping on the Move."*

Sally Symes worked for many years as a designer of children's books before turning her skills to writing them. Her collaborations with Nick Sharratt have won several awards, including The Educational Writers' Award for *The Gooey, Chewy, Rumble, Plop Book* and The Southampton Favourite Book to Share Award for *Something Beginning With Blue.* She works from a shed in Sussex, U.K., accompanied by her grumpy cat. *Sally's stories: "Sleeping Champions," "Record-breaking Beds," "Night Hunters," "The Great Sleep Escape," "Watery Beds," "How Do They Sleep?," "A Grizzly Bear's Winter," "Remarkable Hibernators," and "Lullabies Around the World."*

ILLUSTRATORS

Amy Grimes is an illustrator based in London, U.K., whose work is full of brightly colored elements and soft textures, reflecting the natural patterns found in her subjects. Amy's work is created digitally, using a variety of hand-painted textures, which are scanned and assembled to create digital collages. *Amy illustrated the cover and pages 166–81.*

Anneli Bray is an illustrator based in the northwest of England. From an early age, she could be found painting stories about animals and magical creatures, making books about ponies, and reading voraciously. Since then she has graduated with a First in Illustration, been a bookseller, and traveled to the other side of the world. Anneli has continued to illustrate stories influenced by her love of animals and adventure. *Anneli illustrated pages 118–49.*

Christine Cuddihy is an illustrator based in Leamington Spa, U.K., with a degree in Fine Art. Christine primarily works digitally, with a love of texture, color, and mark-making. She lives amongst a ginormous collection of children's books, with her husband and their beloved hamster, and can never say no to a slice of cake. *Christine illustrated pages 38–53 and 182–5.*

Jacqui Lee's illustrations are focused on storytelling and are inspired by the world around her. Her work aims to bring a smile to people's faces. She loves the handmade, textural look of gouache paint, and always carries a sketchbook with her. An alumni of the Alberta University of the Arts and from Canada, she now lives in London, U.K. *Jacqui illustrated pages 22–37.*

Joanne Liu majored in Graphic Design at the University of Michigan. She received a special mention from the 2018 Bologna Ragazzi Book Awards for her first children's book, *My Museum.* Her second book, *My City,* came out in 2019. *Joanne illustrated pages 86–101 and page 192.*

Katie Rewse is an illustrator based in Bournemouth, U.K., where she studied for both her BA and MA in Illustration. Katie finds inspiration in the outdoors, travel, and adventure. When she is not drawing, she enjoys exploring the coast with her husband in their RV. *Katie illustrated pages 102–17.*

Katie Wilson lives and works in a little old railway house in the beautiful South Island of New Zealand. She creates artwork for both adults and children, and her illustrations are sweet and cheerful with a handmade feel. *Katie illustrated pages 70–85.*

Maddy Vian is an illustrator and art director living by the sea in Kent, U.K. She graduated with an Illustration Animation degree and has worked on a wide variety of creative projects from children's books to music videos. Maddy mixes digital work with handmade textures to make playful imagery. She loves to create work that celebrates positivity, diversity, and reflects her ethical stances. *Maddy illustrated pages 6–21.*

Natalie Smillie is an illustrator based in Devon, U.K. She takes influence from her dog walks throughout the southwest, and in the plants and countryside animals that live around her. She loves reinventing covers for famous books. She paints digitally but she likes to use traditional brushes to create texture and depth in her work. *Natalie illustrated pages 54–69.*

Olivia Holden is an illustrator from Lancashire, U.K. Since graduating, she has worked on a variety of book projects, with this being her first voyage looking into outer space. Her process includes a mix of gouache, pencils, and crayons to create different textures and bring an organic painterly playfulness to her work. *Olivia illustrated pages 150–65.*

Glossary

amphibian: A cold-blooded animal (such as a frog or toad) that has a backbone and usually lives in water when young but on land as an adult

astronaut: A person who travels in space in a spaceship

astronomer: A person who studies outer space and the objects in it

axis: An imaginary straight line around which something (such as a planet) rotates

crater: a hole left in the surface of a planet or moon by a large impact

galaxy: a very large group of stars, gas, and dust in space

gravity: a force that pulls things on the surface of the Earth towards its center

hemisphere: one half of the Earth

lullaby: a song for helping a baby or child fall asleep

lunar: having to do with the Moon

mammal: a warm-blooded animal that has a backbone, feeds its young with milk produced by the mother, and has skin that is mostly covered with hair

Milky Way: a wide band of light that stretches across the sky and is caused by the light from a great number of stars

mucus: thick, slippery, sticky stuff that coats parts of the body to moisten and protect it

observatory: a place that has instruments (such as telescopes) for observing objects in space

orbit: the path that a body in space takes in moving around another body

oxygen: a chemical element necessary for life that is found in the air as a gas with no taste or smell

planet: a large body in space that orbits a star, such as the Sun

predator: an animal that gets food mostly by killing and eating other animals

prey: an animal that is hunted and killed by another animal for food

primate: an animal that belongs to a group of mammals, including apes, monkeys, and humans

Rapid Eye Movement (REM) sleep: a period of sleep when a person is dreaming that is characterized by quick movement of the eyes

rocket: a vehicle that is propelled by a jet engine

satellite: [1] a body in space that revolves around a planet [2] an object or vehicle sent into space to revolve around the Earth, Moon, or a planet

savannah: land in warm parts of the world (such as Africa) that is covered with grass and only a few trees and shrubs

solar system: the Sun and the planets, asteroids, comets, and meteors that revolve around it

species: a group of living things that share common characteristics and are able to produce young with one another

star: any of the bodies in space except planets that can be seen at night and that look like points of light in the sky that do not move

universe: everything on Earth and in space when thought of as making up one system

womb: an organ in the body of a female mammal where the young develop before being born

Definitions courtesy of Merriam-Webster.

Sources

All the pages in this book have been fact-checked by the team at Britannica, and the authors have drawn from the articles on britannica.com in their research. They have also consulted numerous other publications and articles, and would like to acknowledge the following key sources in the making of this book:

WEBSITES

www.astronomy.com

www.bbc.com

www.bear.org/brown-grizzly-bear-facts

www.britishmuseum.org

www.guinnessworldrecords.com

www.ice.org.uk

www.iwm.org.uk

www.mathshistory.st-andrews.ac.uk

www.mhs.ox.ac.uk

www.nasa.gov

www.nationalgeographic.com

www.nhs.uk

www.ripleys.com

www.smithsonianmag.com

www.tideway.london/the-tunnel

BOOKS

Bryson, Bill, *The Body: A Guide for Occupants* (Doubleday, 2019)

Hawass, Zahi, *Tutankhamun: The Treasures of the Tomb* (Thames & Hudson, 2018)

Morton, Oliver, *The Moon: A History for the Future* (Economist Books, 2019)

Ridpath, Ian, *Astronomy: A Visual Guide* (Dorling Kindersley, 2018)

Walker, Matthew, *Why We Sleep: The New Science of Sleep and Dreams* (Scribner, 2018)

Index

A

aboriginal people 163
Africa 25, 30, 47, 51, 96, 100, 163, 181
Alaska 119, 143, 147
ancient Egyptians 18, 38, 41, 42
ancient Greeks 162
Asia 47, 96, 100
    Southeast Asia 92
astronaut 27, 54–9, 174–7
aurora australis, see
    Southern Lights
aurora borealis, see
    Northern Lights
Australia 117, 135, 142

B

babies 14, 70, 73, 74–5, 108, 125, 182
baker 84–5
bats 24, 90–1
Batammaliba people 181
bathroom 55, 58, 76
bears 118–9
    grizzly 118–9, 120–5
bed-stove 52–3
Bible, the 18, 145
blanket 53, 122
blood Moon 178–9
British Museum, London, U.K. 18, 113
bugs 90, 92, 96–7
bumblebees 126
burrow 94, 96, 98, 100, 112, 123, 130, 132–3, 139
bus 68–9, 78

C

cats 24, 100–1

caves 24, 30–1, 90, 122
Central America 47, 60, 116
charpoy 46
children 6, 12, 13, 20, 50
China 18, 37, 52, 94, 144, 180
constellations 160–1, 162
cosmonaut 27, 54, 174
cows 40, 80, 114, 144

D

den 122–3, 125
diurnal 139
dolphins 106–7, 111
dreams 8, 14–19, 37, 69
    daydream 103
    dreamcatcher 19
ducks 66, 110, 111,

E

eclipse 181
    lunar eclipse 178–9, 181
elephants 25, 29, 114
exercise 6, 21, 56, 139

F

fall 120, 147, 172
farmer 80, 82
feathers 87, 89
fish 81, 82–3
    parrotfish 104
fishers 82
flamingos 114
four-poster bed 32–3
frigate birds 111
frogs 92, 128–9
fur 51, 89, 101, 108–9, 116, 119
futon 46, 53

G

Galileo Galilei 157, 158, 159, 172–3, 174
giraffes 115, 163
groundhogs 132–3
Guinness World Records 22–3, 28

H

hammocks 60–1, 62, 63
headrest 41, 51; see also pillow
hemispheres 160–1, 163
hibernation 126–33
Hopi people 144
horses 66, 114, 162, 183
hospital 70–5

I

igloo 51
Inca people 181
International Space Station (ISS) 54–7, 176
Inuit 51

K

koalas 117
Korowai people 48

L

ladybugs 126, 134
larks 7
long-eared jerboas 94–5, 101
lullabies 21, 182–5
lungfish 130–1

M

Mars 157, 177
mattress 30–1, 44, 46, 47
Mayan people 61
memory 10
mice 86, 87, 94, 120
Milky Way 155, 163
Moon 86, 137, 156, 165,
    166–71, 172–7, 178–81
    blood moon 178–9
    far side 170–1, 176
    phases 171
mosquitoes 24, 30, 47, 48

N

narrowboat 66
night hunters 86–7, 92–3
nocturnal 7, 86, 90, 92, 98,
    100, 138, 139
North America 24, 119, 127,
    128, 144
Northern Lights 146–9

O

observatory 158–9
Ojibwa people 19
orangutans 29
orbit 27, 54, 141, 170, 176
owls 7, 87–9, 92,

P

pangolins 96–7
parrotfish see fish
pillow 41, 59, 115

Q

quilt 30, 35

R

rapid eye movement (REM)
    8, 15
record breakers 22–3,
    24, 27, 28, 31–7; see also
    Guinness World Records
Russia 26–7, 64–5, 147, 174

S

sea otters 108–9
sewer 76–7
sharks 102–3
sleep talk 13
sleeping bag 59, 104,
sleepwalk 13
sloths 116
snails 113
snakes 19, 60, 94, 101, 132,
    133
snoring 12, 28–9, 53, 72
solar system 149, 151, 166,
    176
solstice 142–5
South America 47, 116, 181
Southern Lights 148–9
spiders 98, 112; see also
    tarantulas
spring 125, 126, 129, 132,
    147
stargazing 156, 164–5
submarine 67
summer 34, 122, 125, 138,
    140, 141, 142, 143,
Sun
    midnight Sun 140, 143
    sunlight 19, 137, 142, 170
    sunrise 56, 83, 134, 137,
        139
    sunset 56, 134, 137
supermarket 80–1

T

tarantulas 98, 112
tarsiers 92–3
telescope 54, 156–9, 172–3,
    174
train 64–6, 69
    train tracks 79
tree house 48
truck 78, 80–1
turtles 127
Tutankhamun 38–44

V

Victoria & Albert Museum,
    London, U.K. 33

W

walruses 105
waterbed 47
whales 106–7
winter 52, 118–9, 122–5,
    126–9, 132–3, 140–5,
    146–7

Z

zebras 114, 163
Zulu people 51
Zuni people 144

BRITANNICA BOOKS

Britannica Books is an imprint of What on Earth Publishing, in collaboration with Britannica, Inc.
Allington Castle, Maidstone, Kent ME16 0NB, United Kingdom
30 Ridge Road Unit B, Greenbelt, Maryland, 20770, United States

First published in the United States in 2020

Developed by Sally Symes
Text by Jackie McCann, Jen Arena, Rachel Valentine, and Sally Symes
Design and Art Direction by Sally Symes
Cover design by Andy Forshaw
Cover illustration by Amy Grimes
Illustrations by Amy Grimes, Anneli Bray, Christine Cuddihy, Jacqui Lee, Joanne Liu,
Katie Rewse, Katie Wilson, Maddy Vian, Natalie Smillie, and Olivia Holden
Index by Corinne Lucas

Encyclopaedia Britannica
Alison Eldridge, Managing Editor; Dennis Skord, Fact Checking Supervisor;
Fia Bigelow, Letricia A. Dixon, Will Gosner, R. E. Green, Fact Checkers.

Britannica Books
Nancy Feresten, Publisher; Natalie Bellos, Executive Editor;
Andy Forshaw, Art Director; Alenka Oblak, Production Manager

Library of Congress Cataloging-in-Publication Data available upon request

ISBN: 9781912920655

Printed and bound in Slovenia
FT/Maribor, Slovenia/11/2021

10 9 8 7 6 5 4 3 2

whatonearthbooks.com
britannica-books.com

NIGHT OWL PAINTING
NIGHT OWL

FSC
www.fsc.org

MIX
Paper from
responsible sources
FSC® C106954

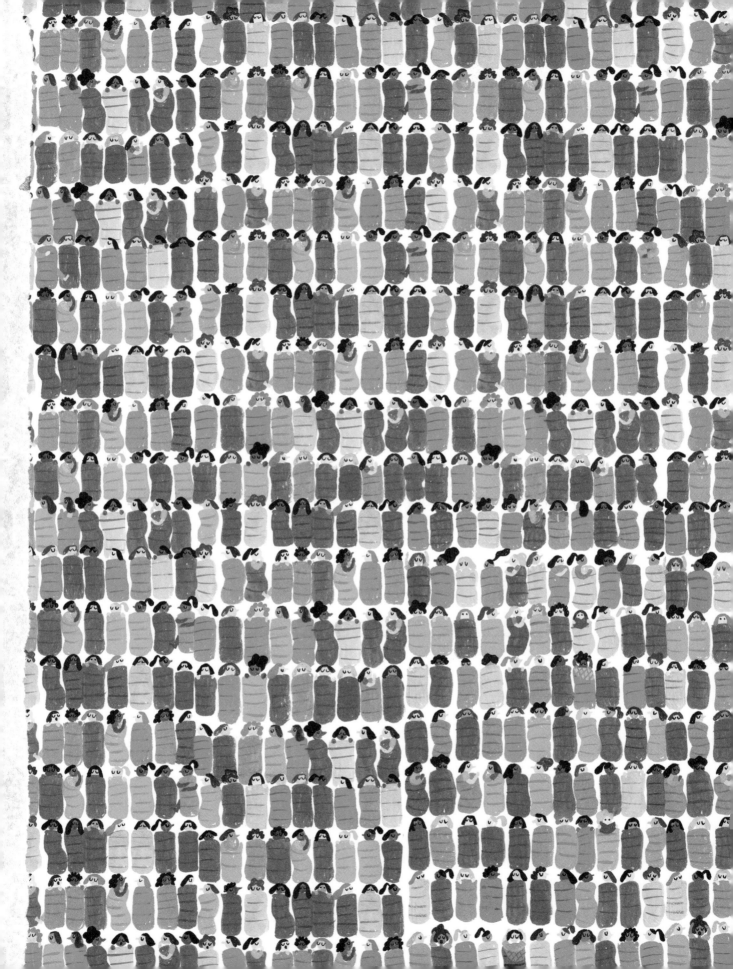